Colorful Critters

This book belongs to:

Copyright © 2021
The rights reserved to the publisher, and it is not allowed
to publish, copy or use any of this book. It is allowed for
personal use only, and it is not allowed for commercial
use

alligator

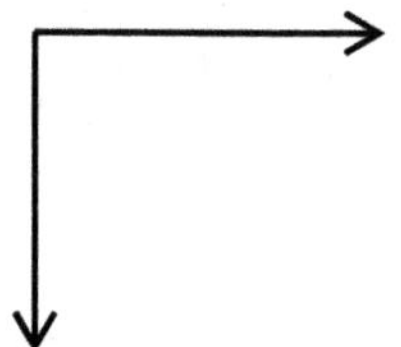

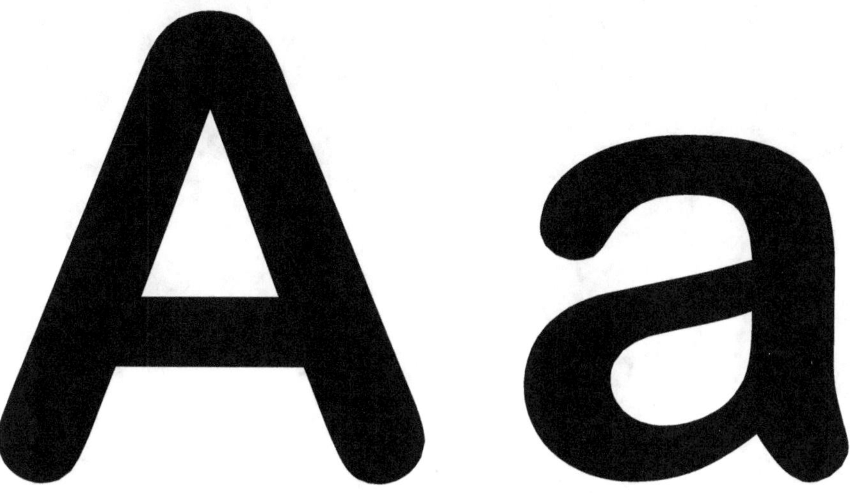

Trace the letter

 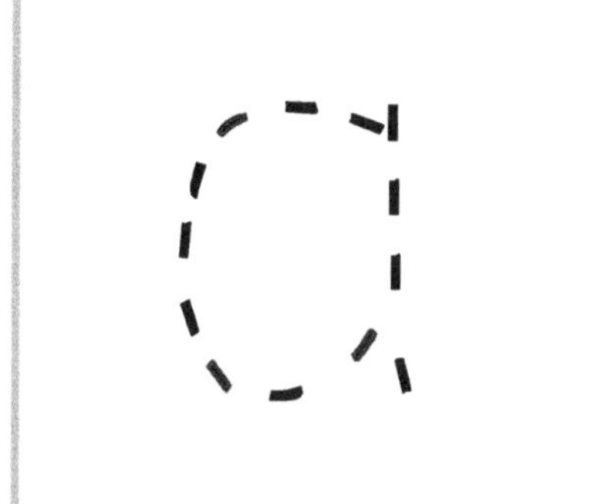 

  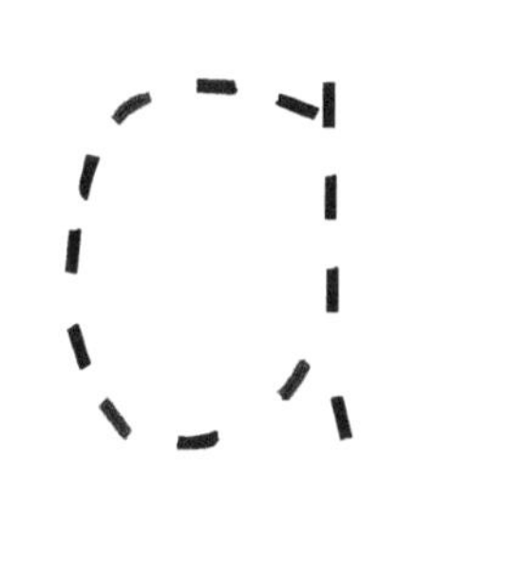

 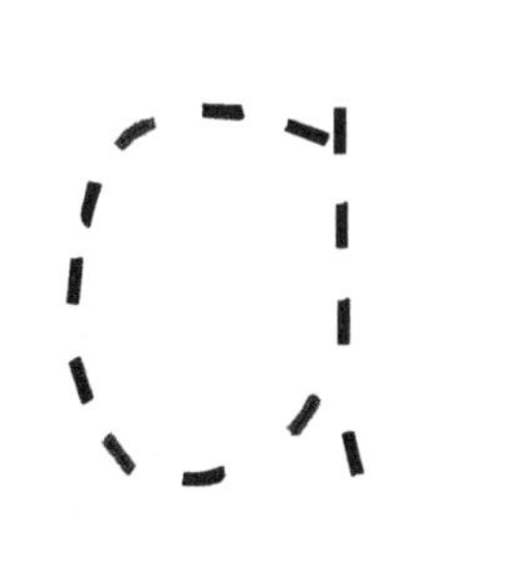 

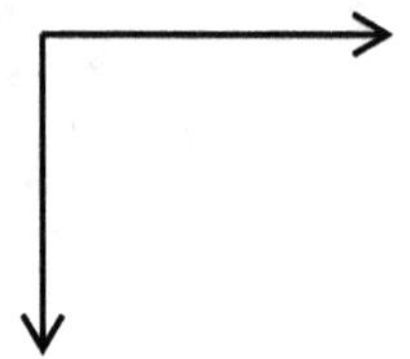

bunny

B b

Trace the letter

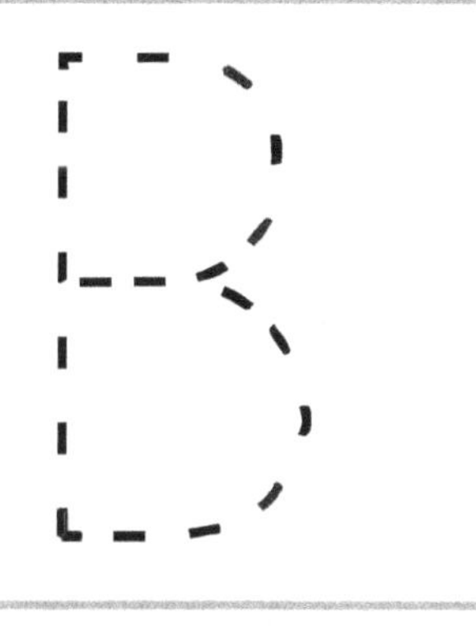 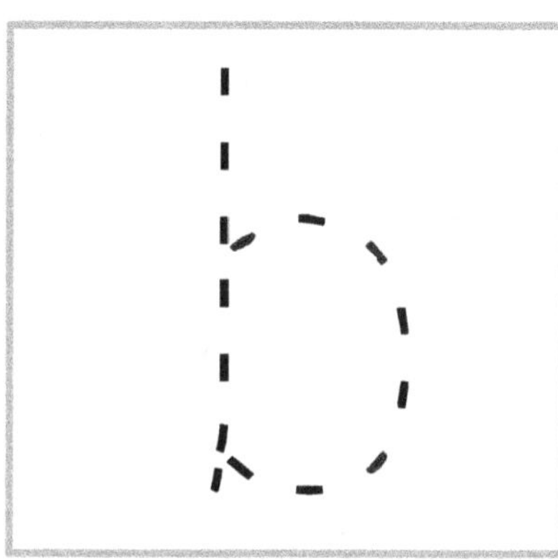 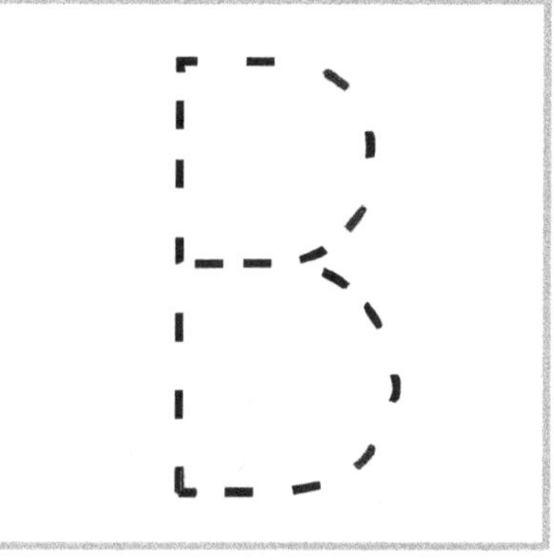

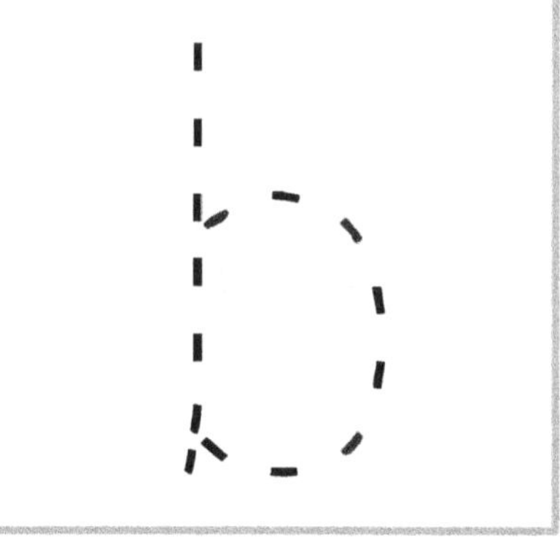 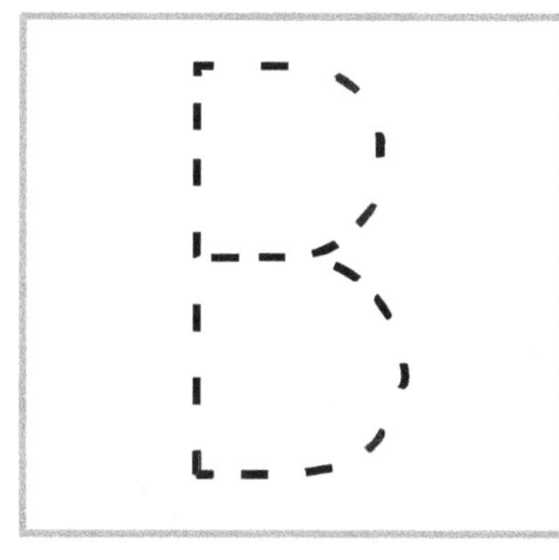 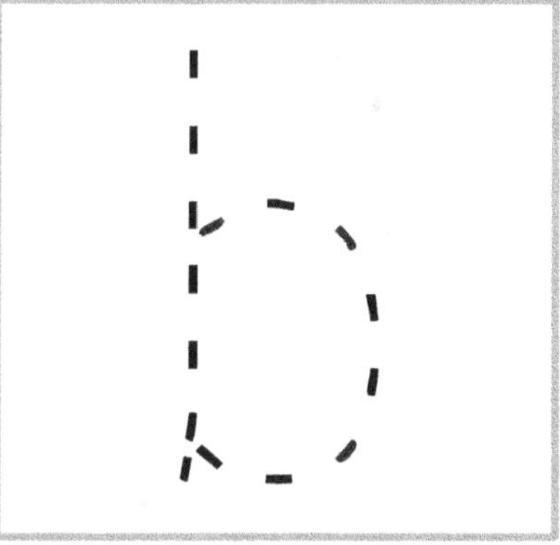

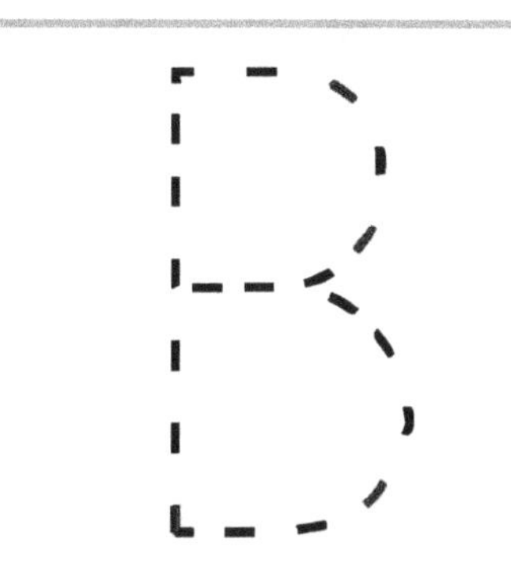 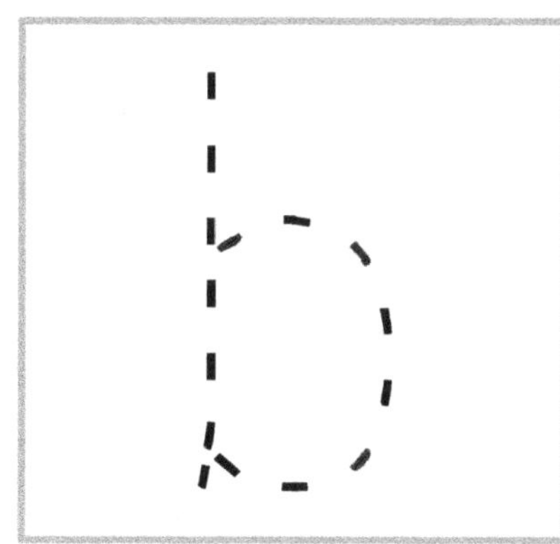 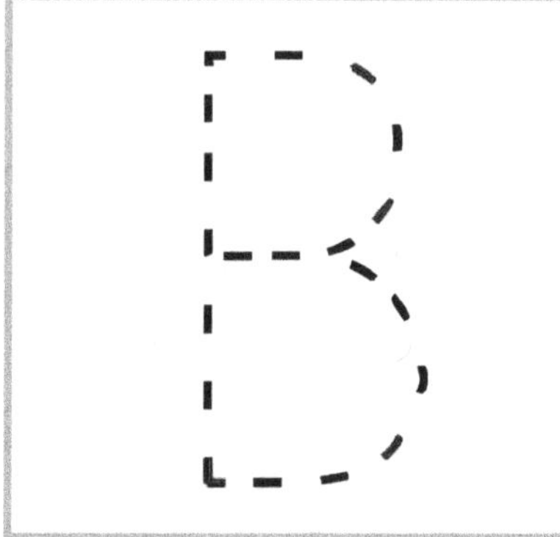

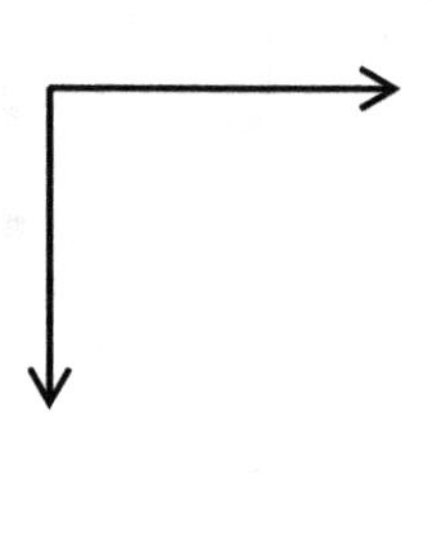

COW

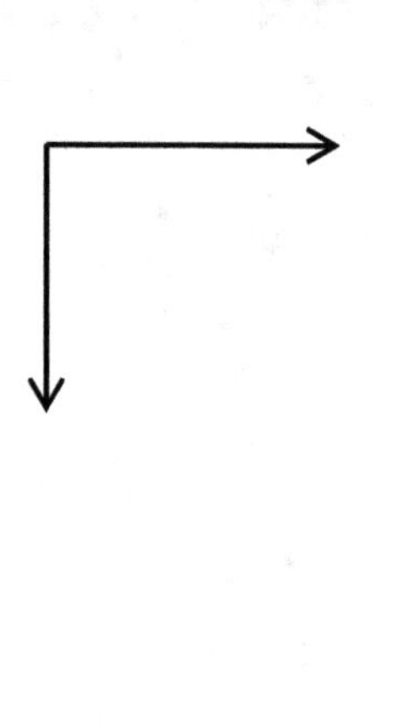

Trace the letter

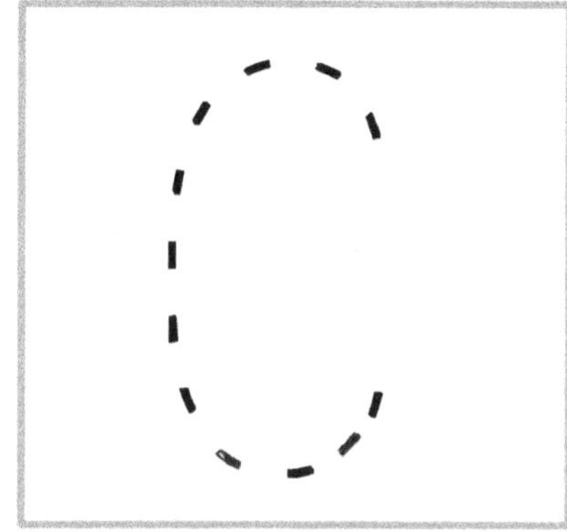  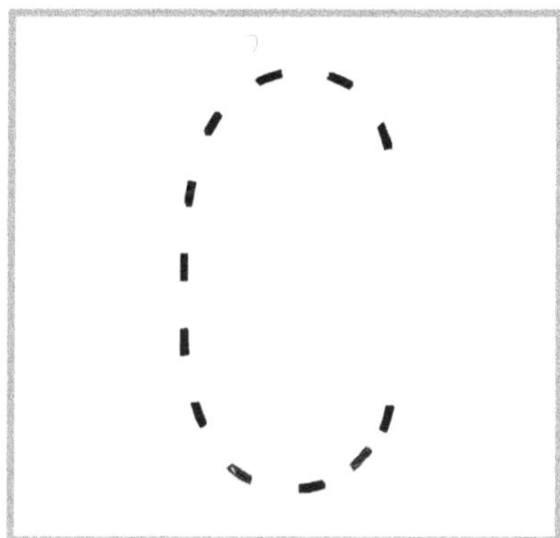

 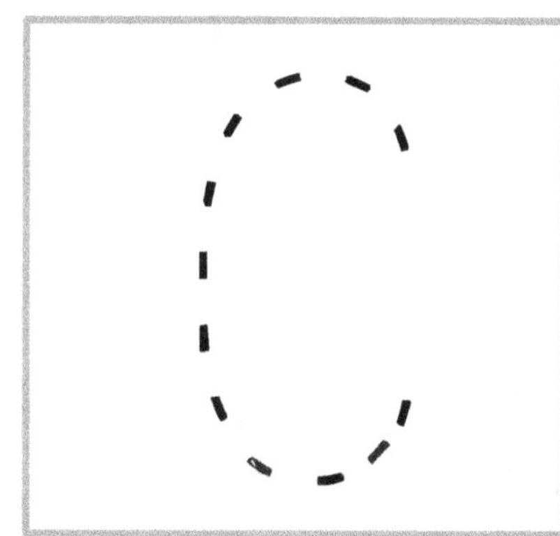 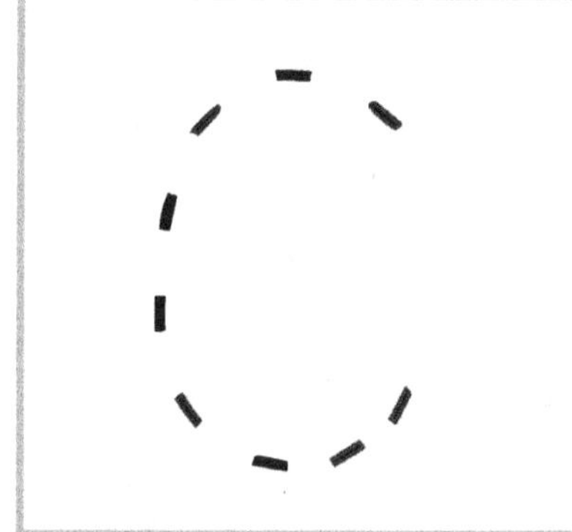

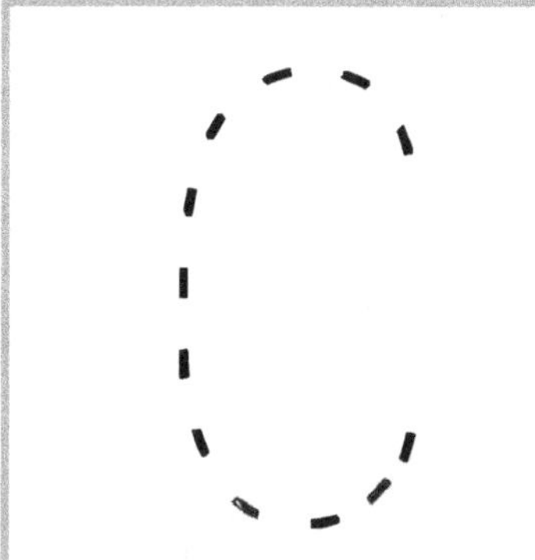 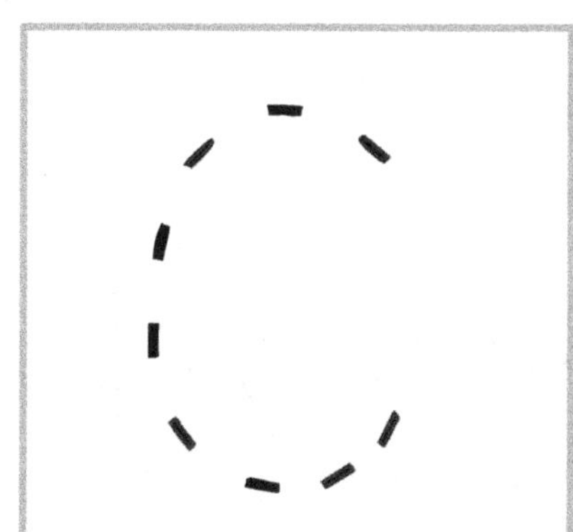 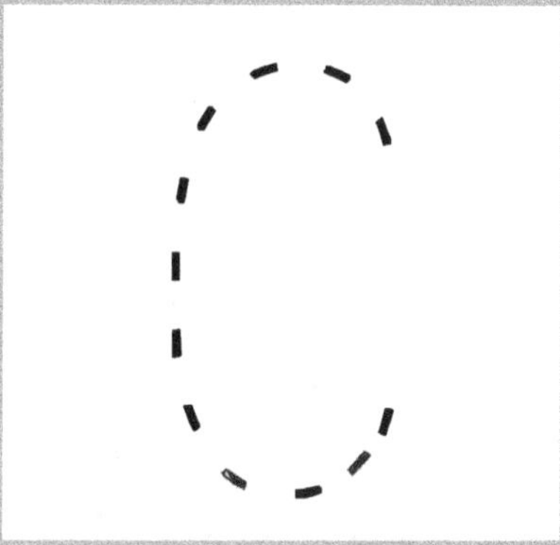

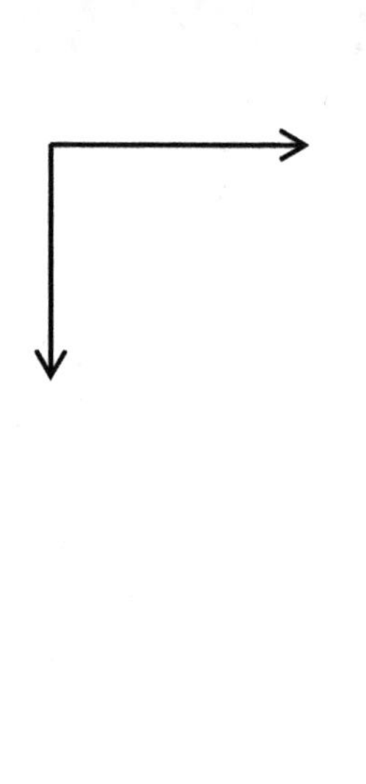

duck

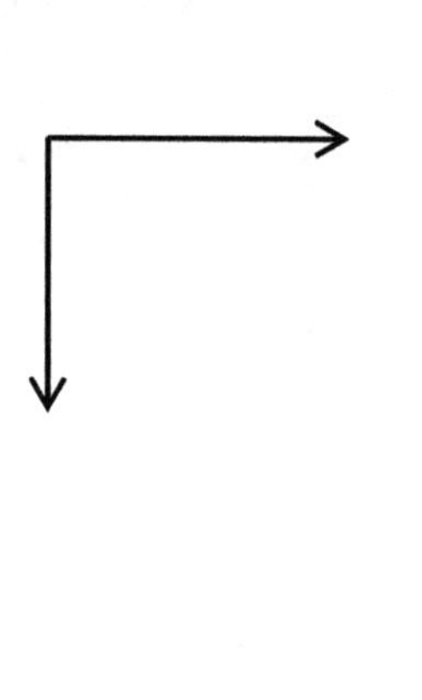

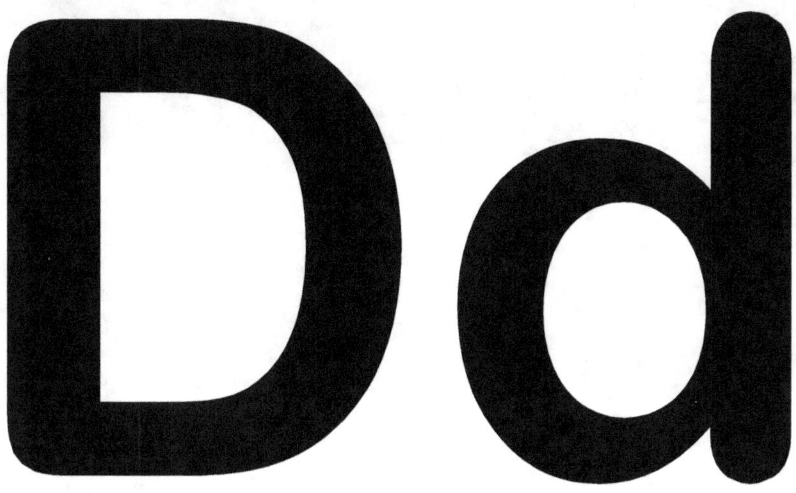

Dd

Trace the letter

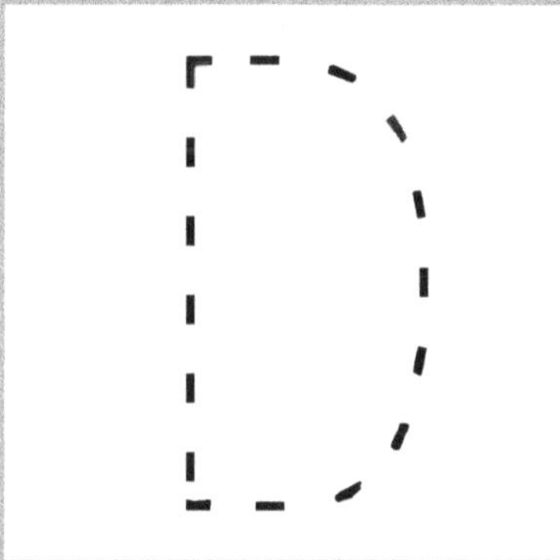 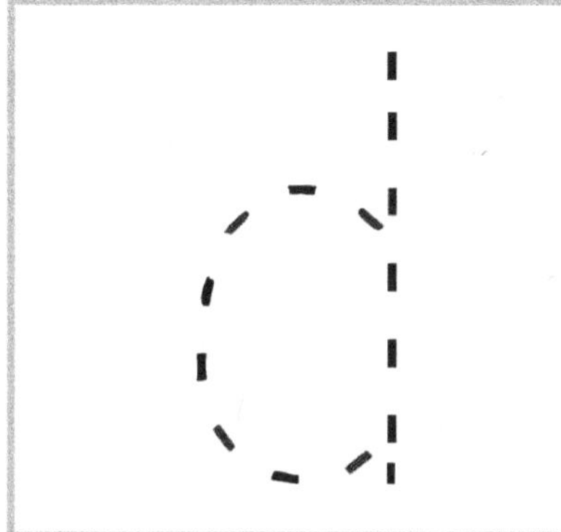 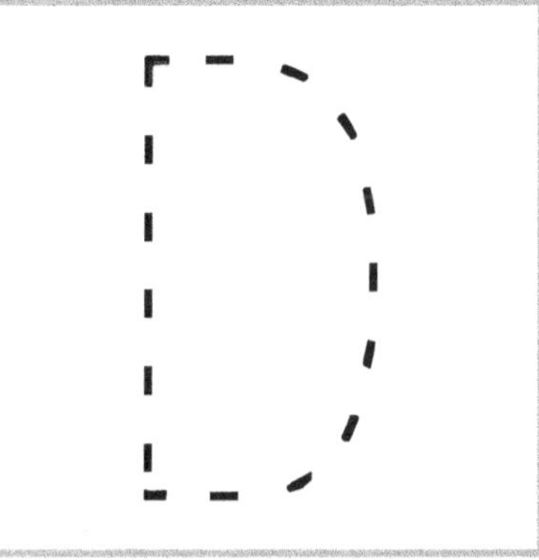

 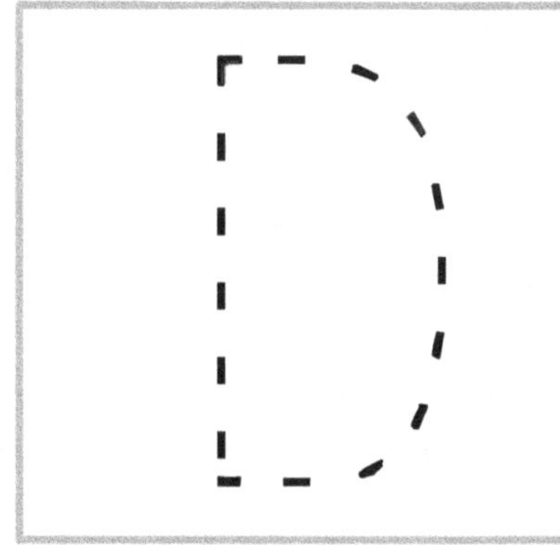 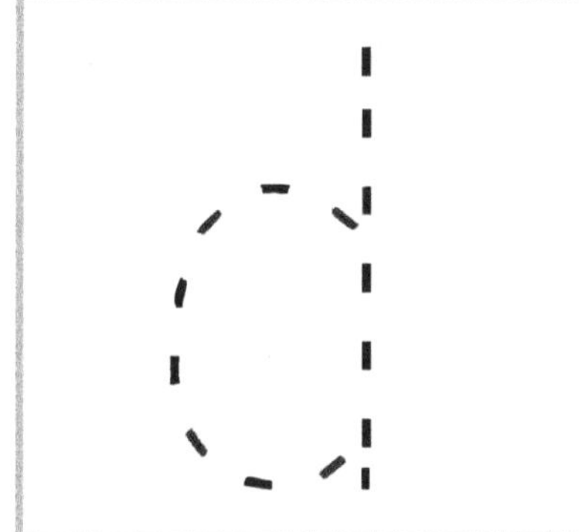

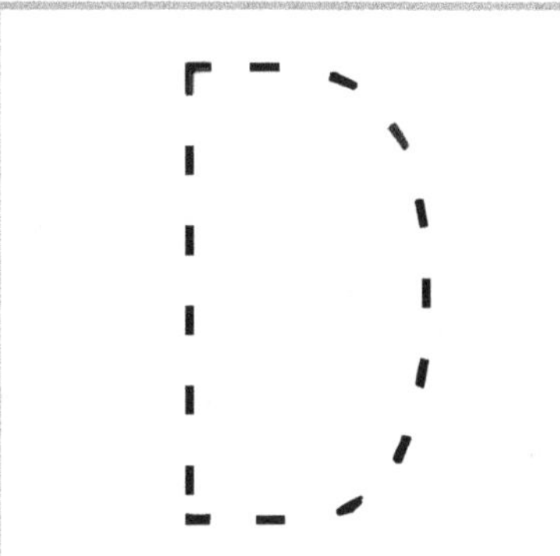 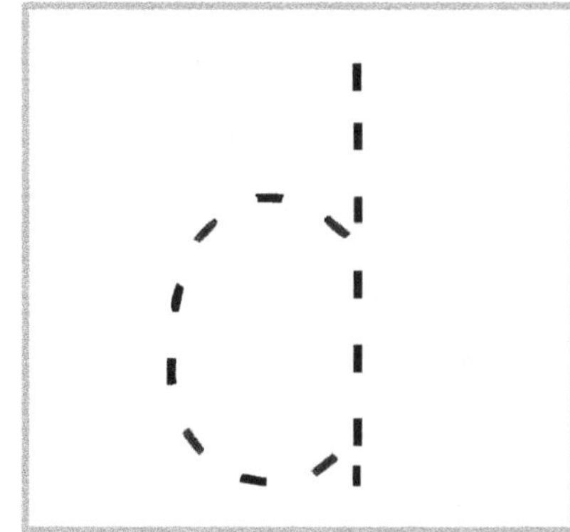

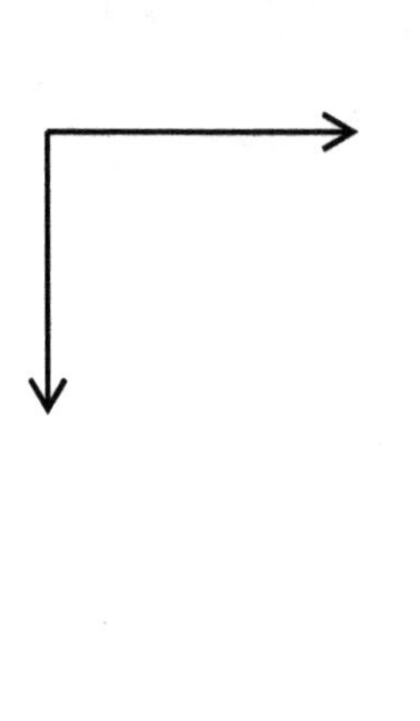

elephant

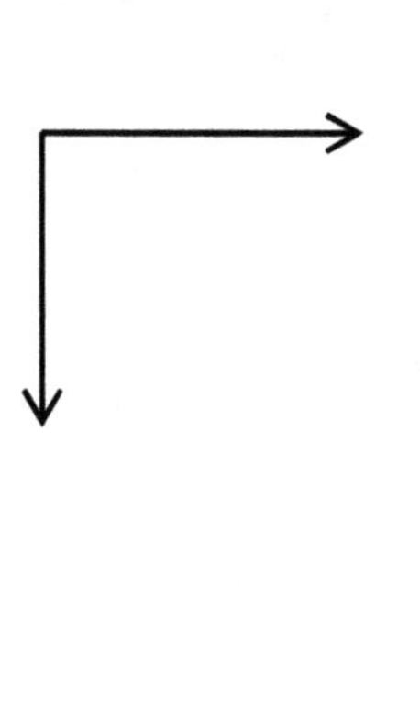

E e

Trace the letter

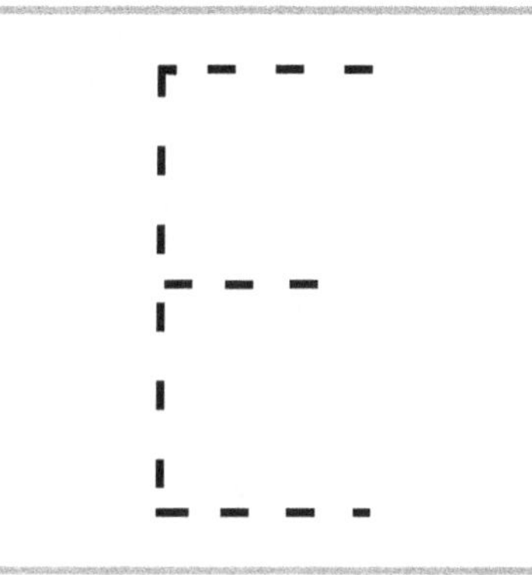

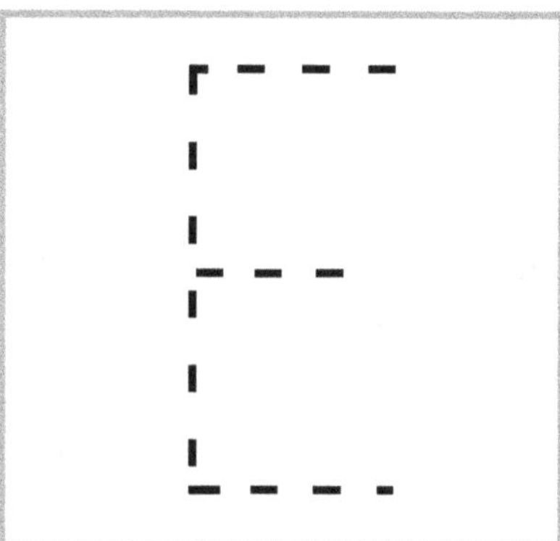

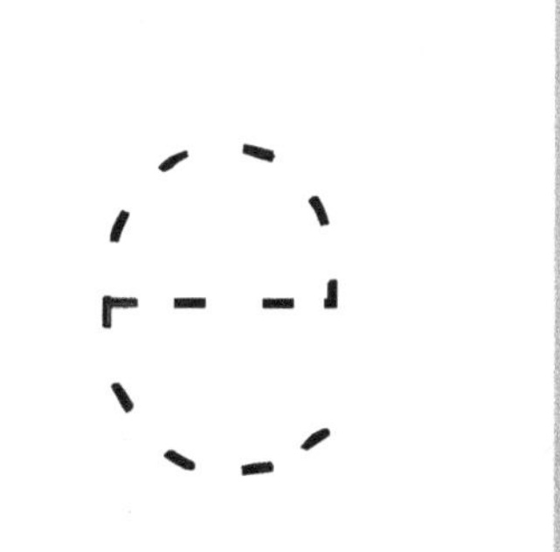

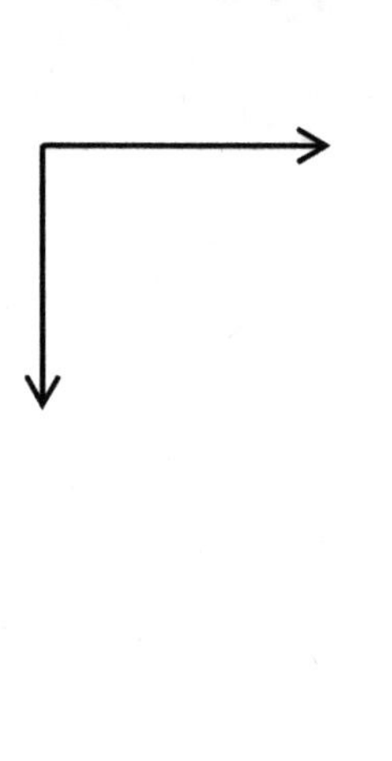

frog

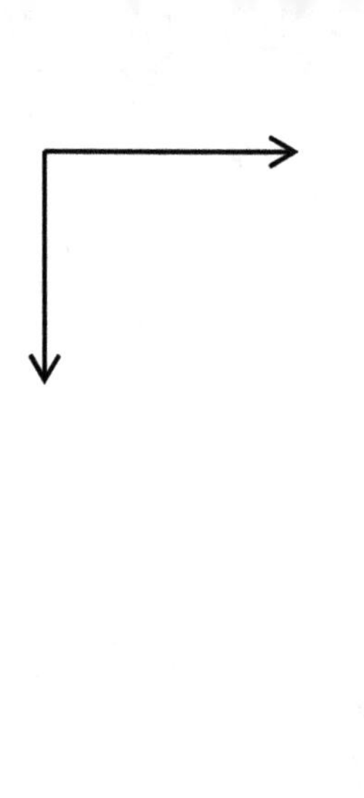

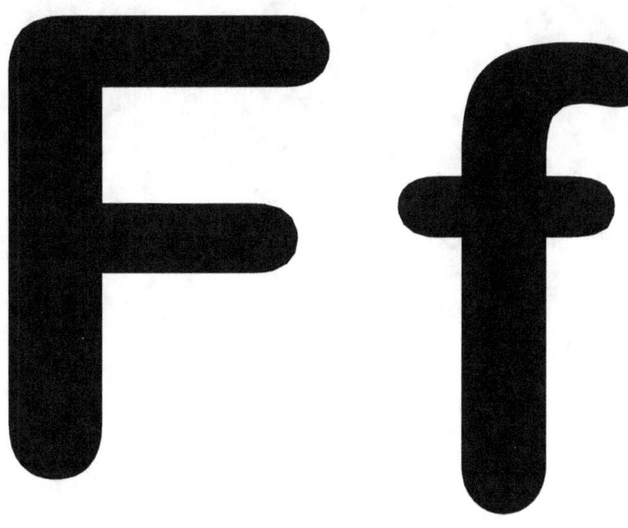

Trace the letter

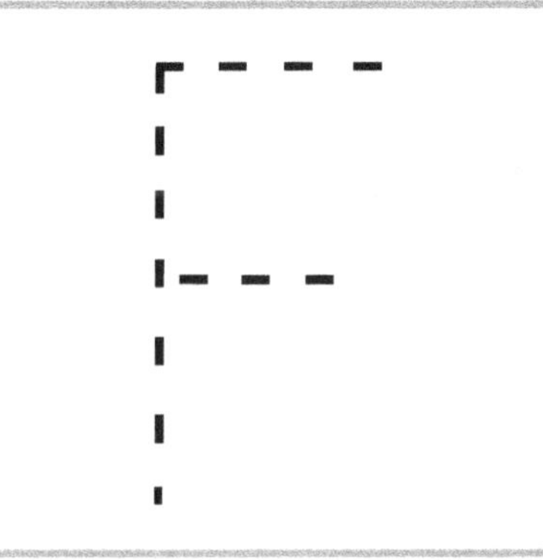

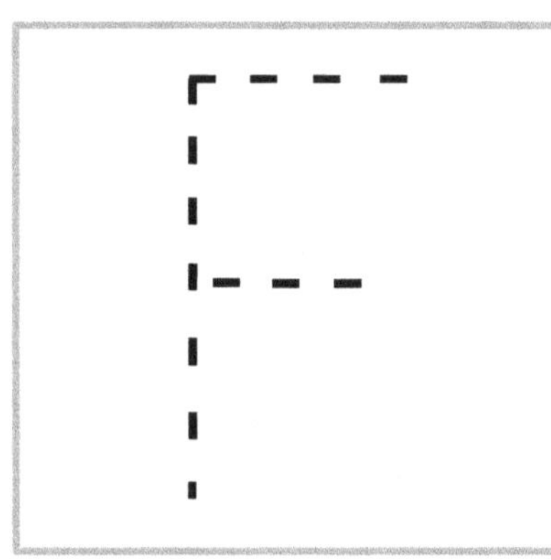

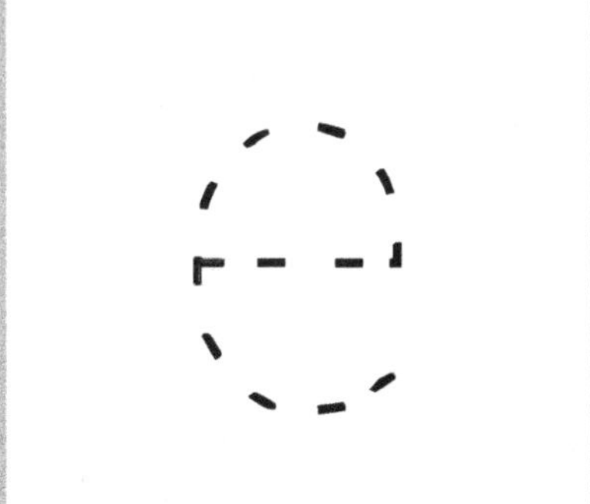

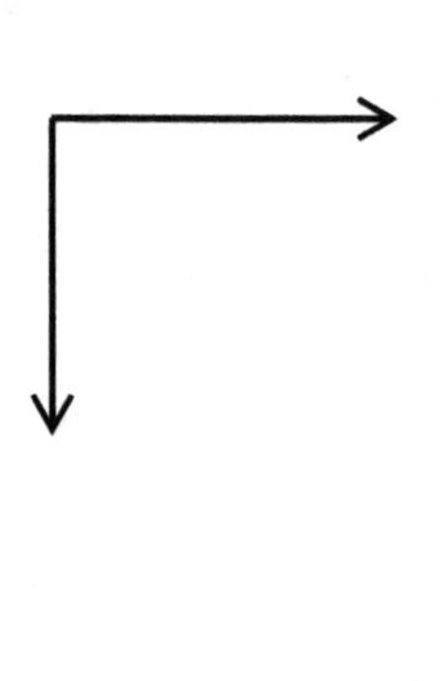

giraffe

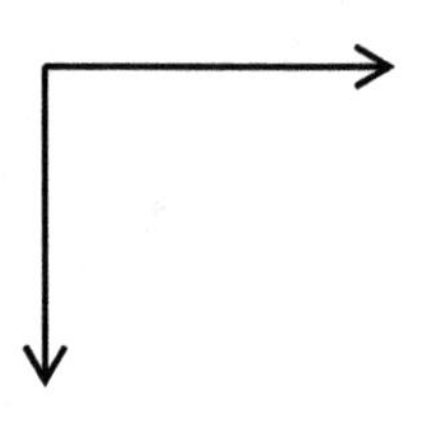

G g

Trace the letter

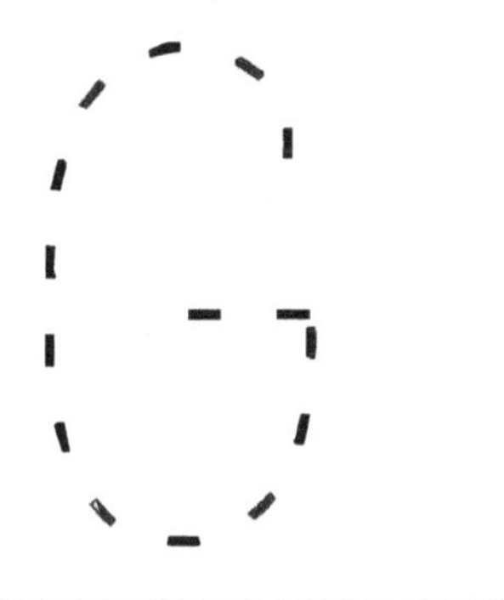 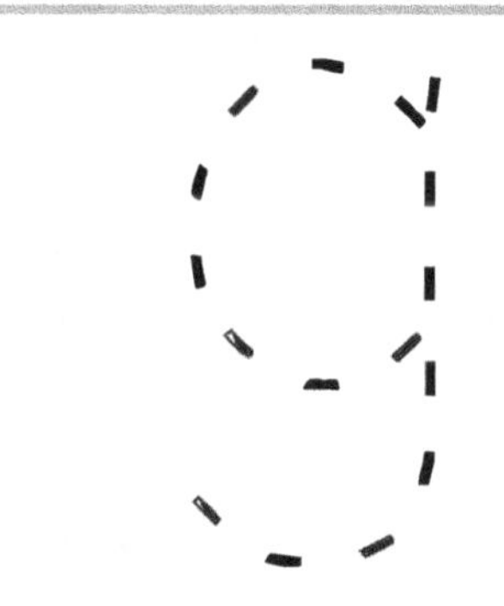 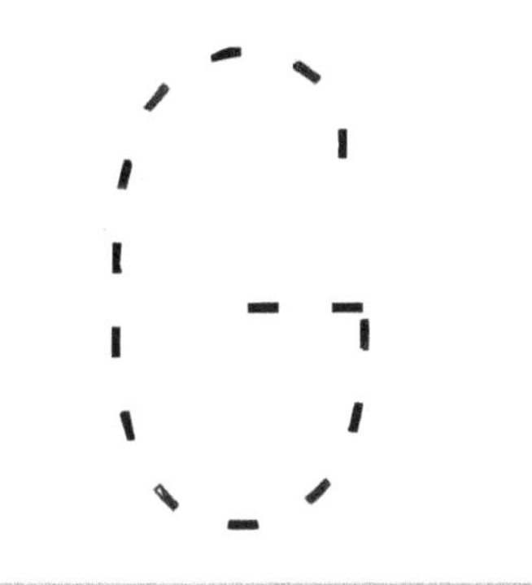

 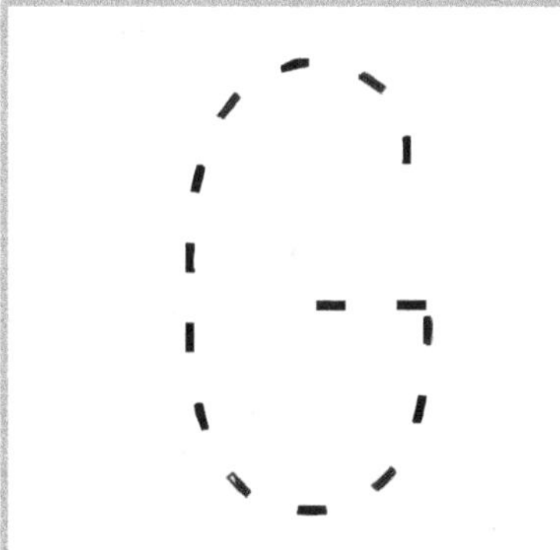 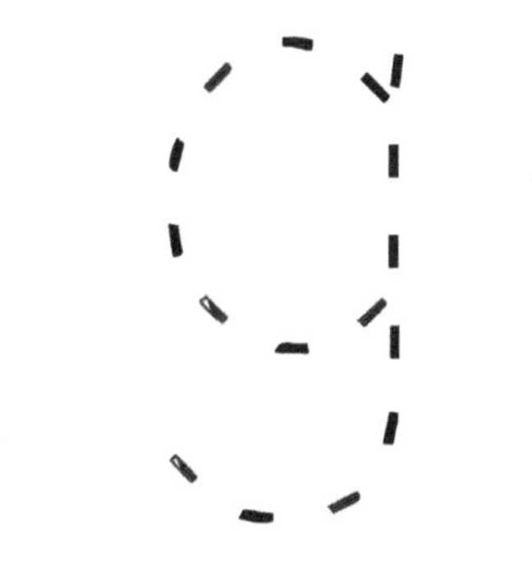

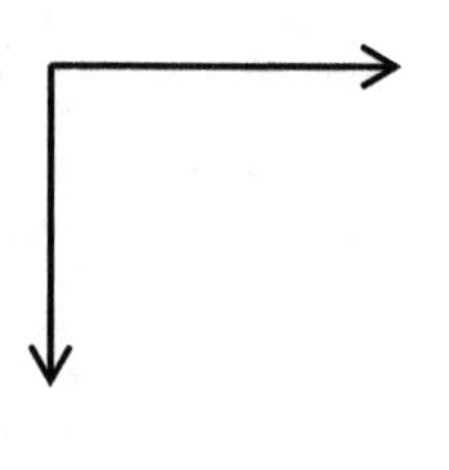

hose

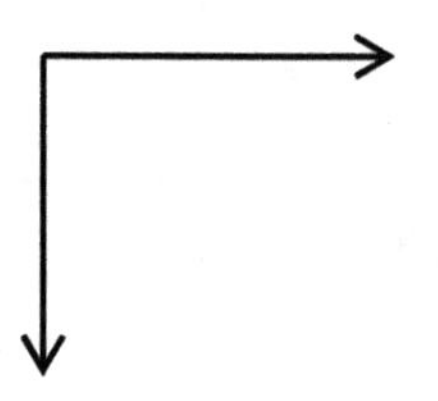

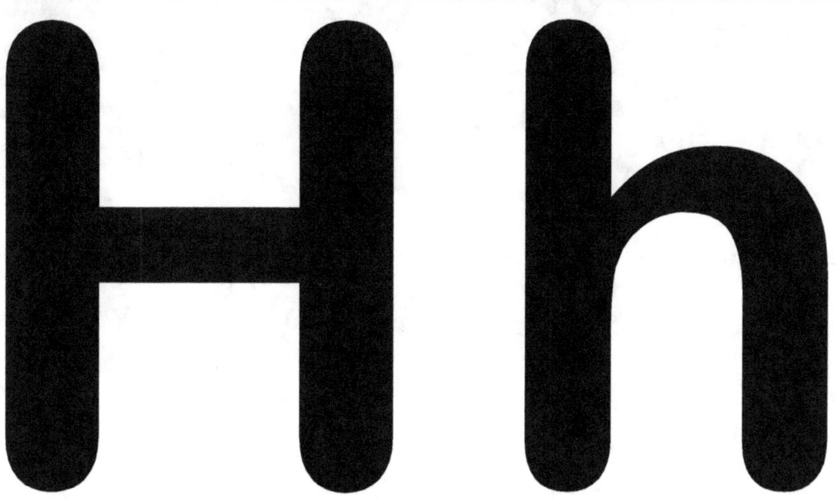

Trace the letter

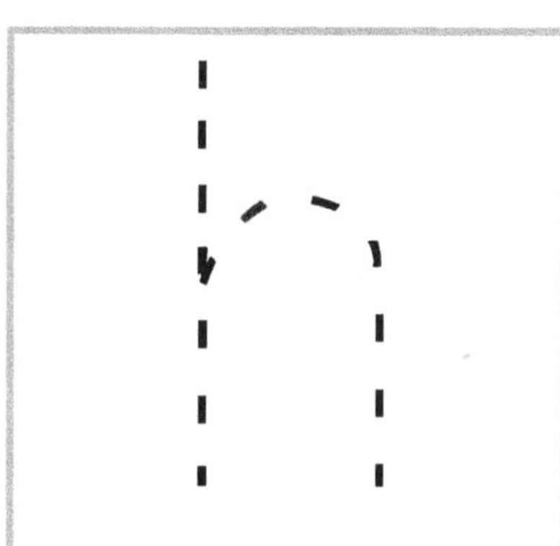 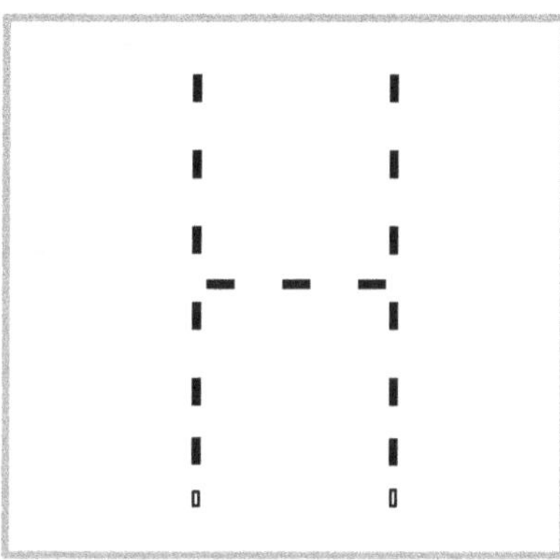

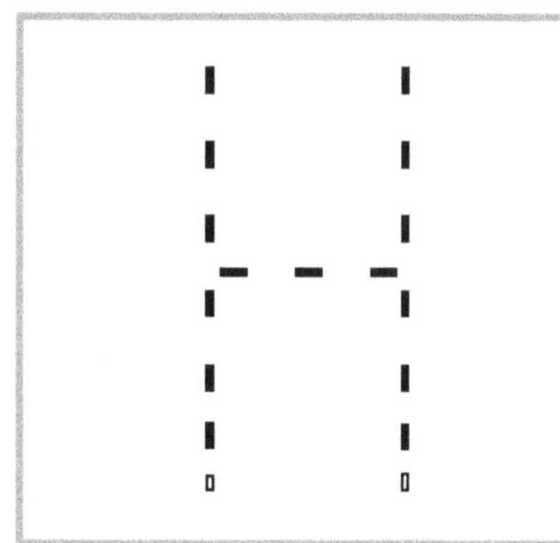

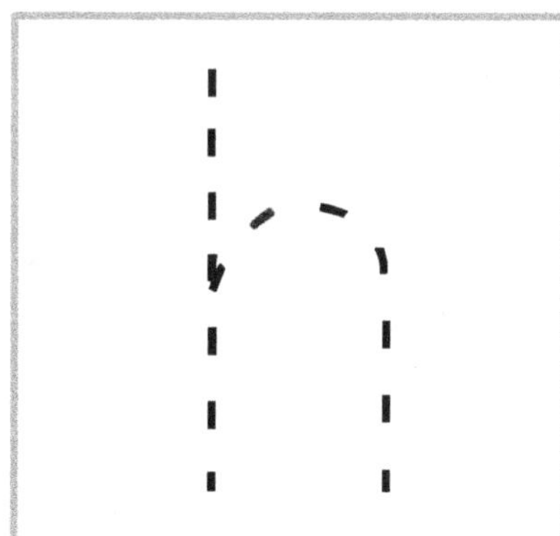

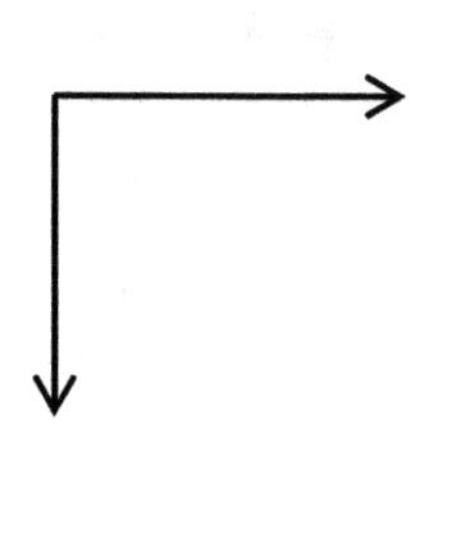

ibis

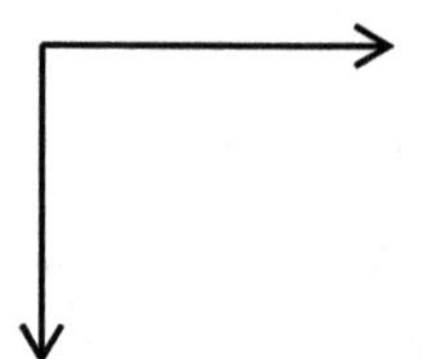

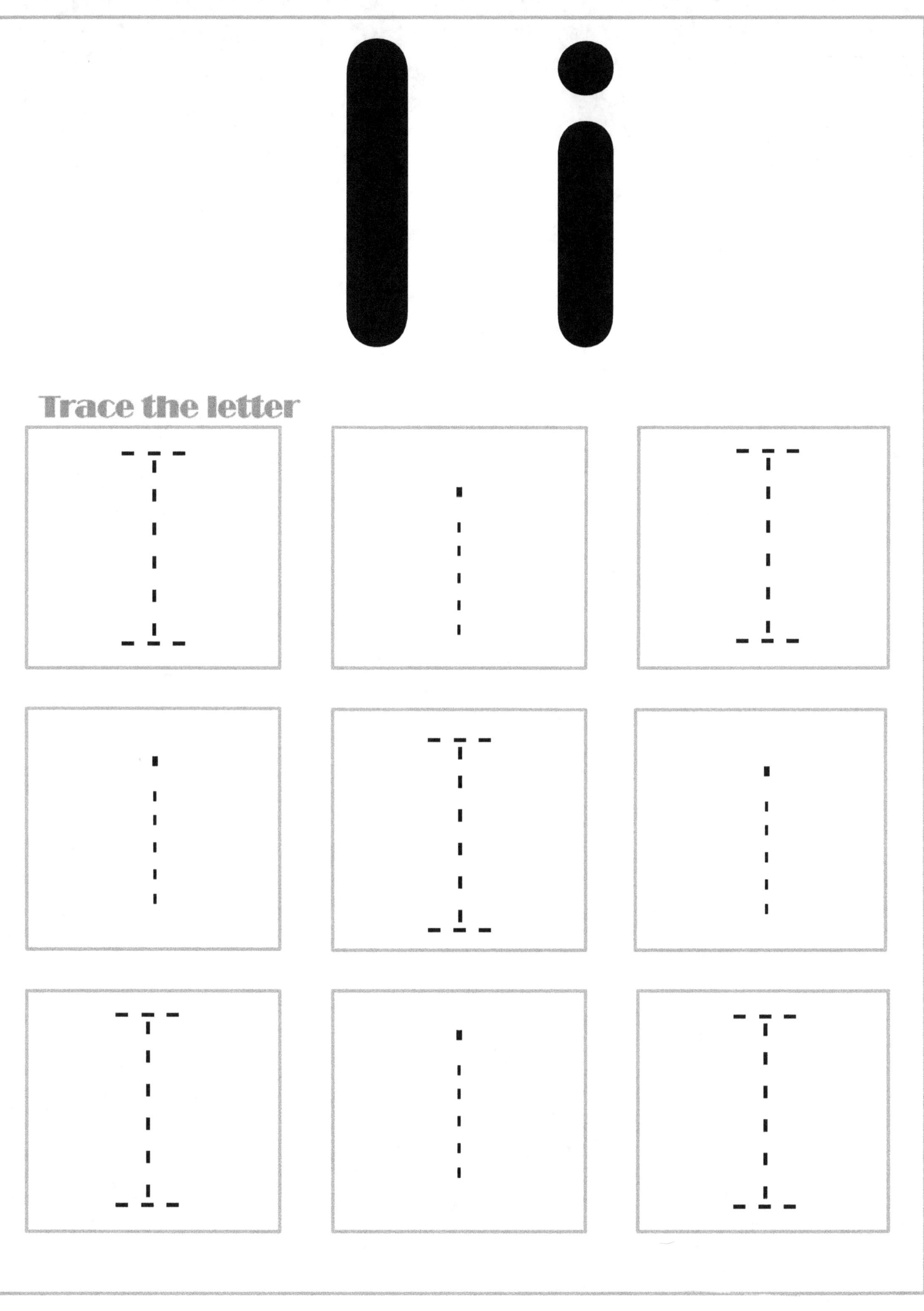

Trace the letter

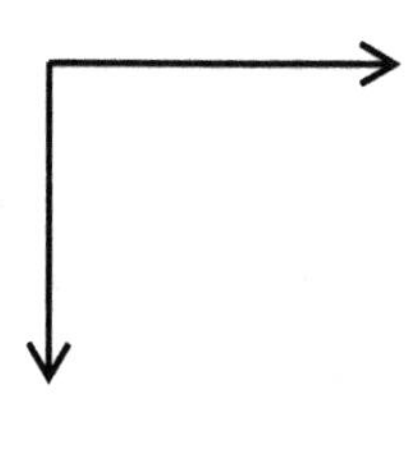

Jellyfish

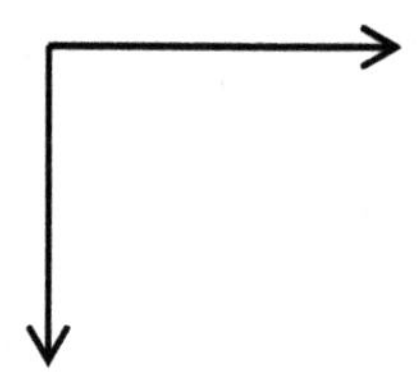

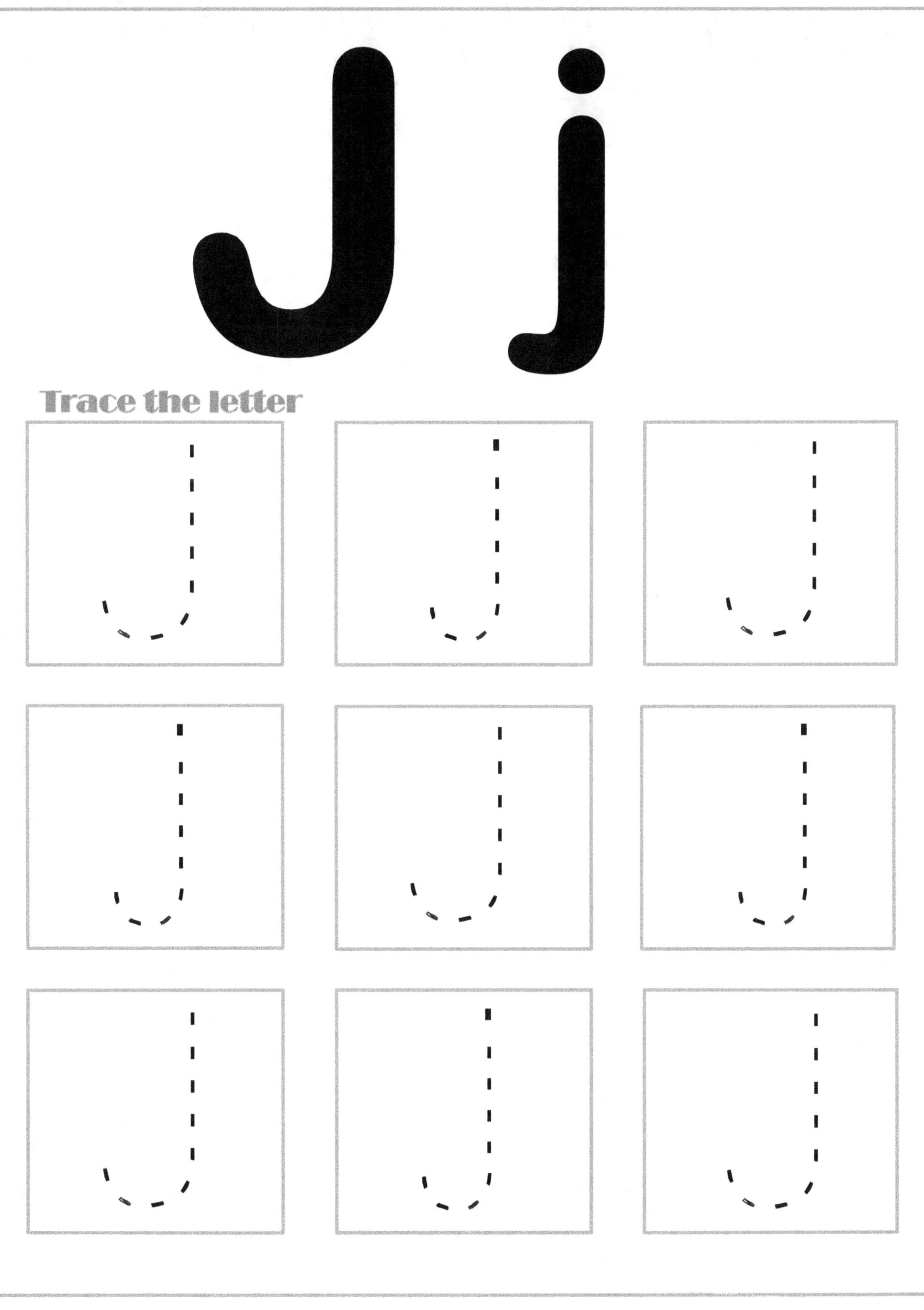
J j
Trace the letter

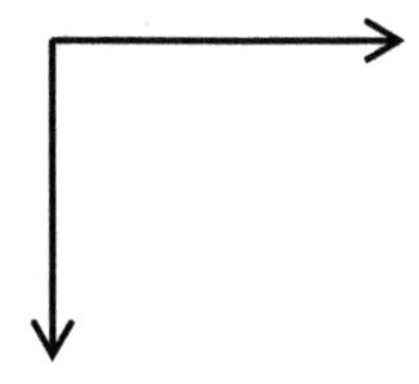

kangaroo

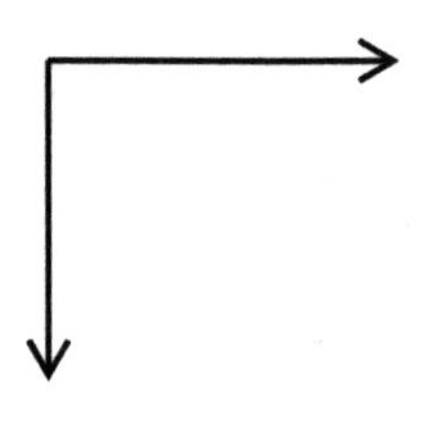

Trace the letter

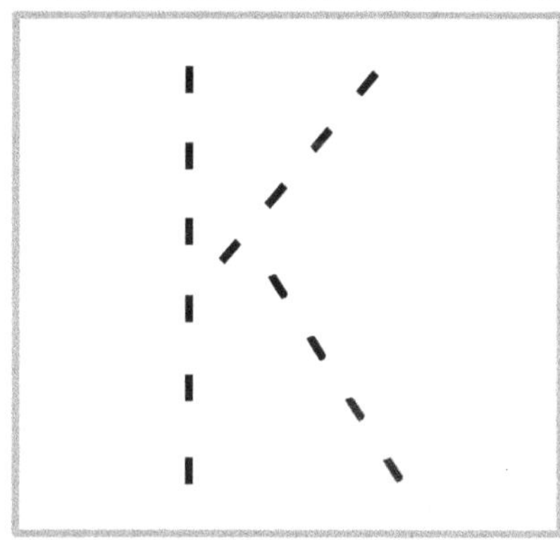 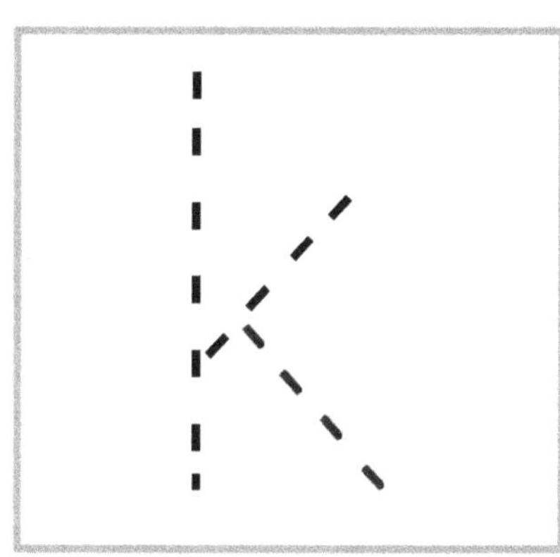 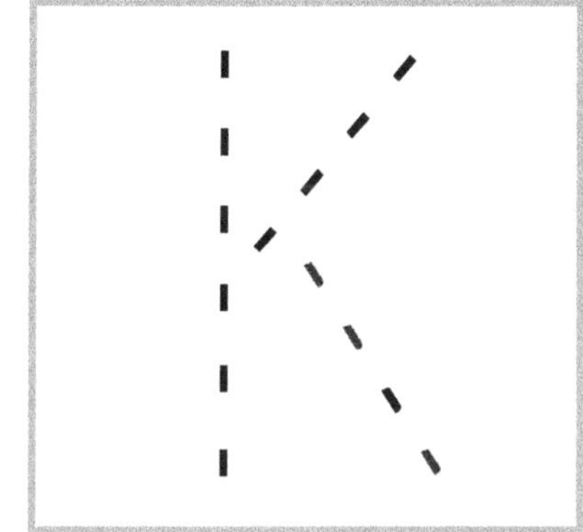

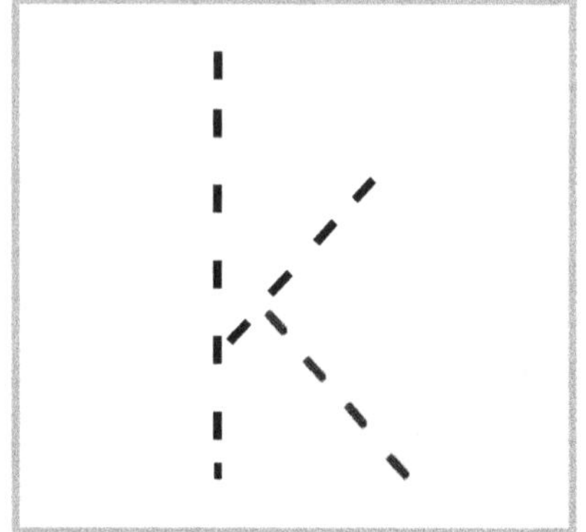 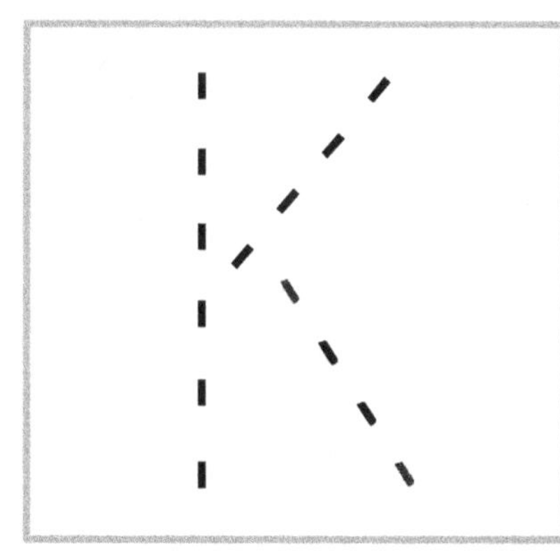 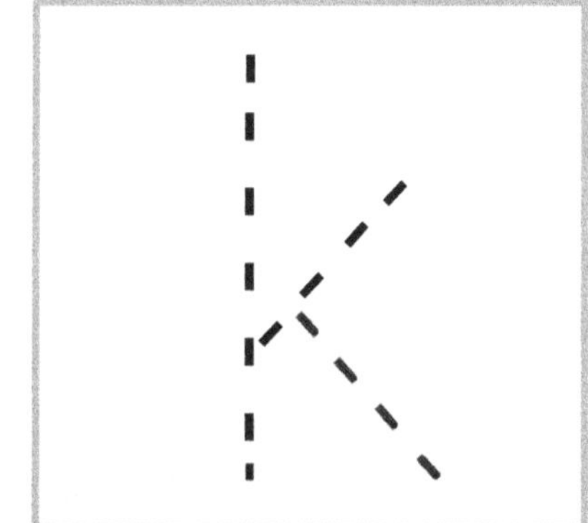

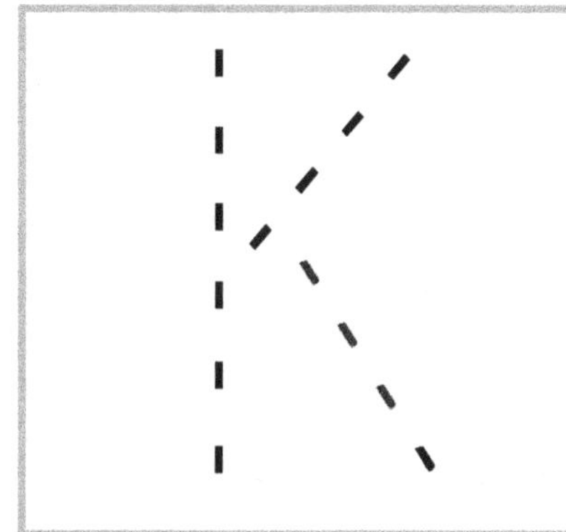 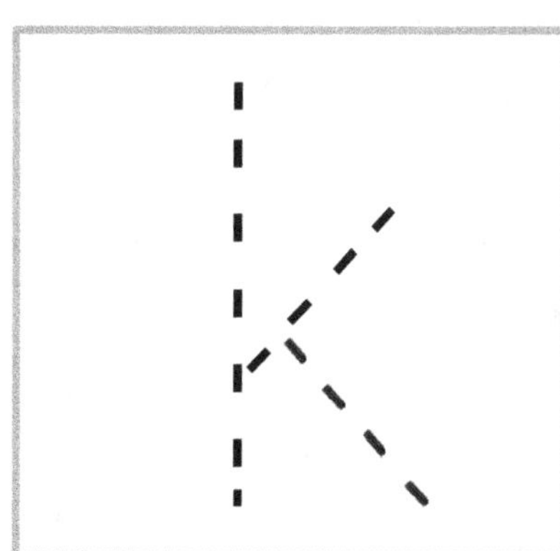 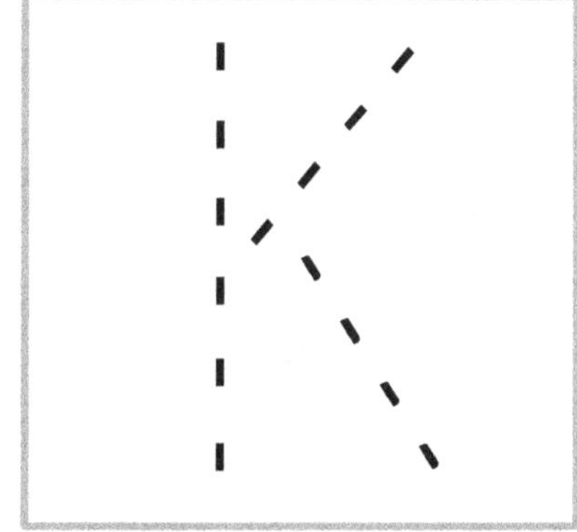

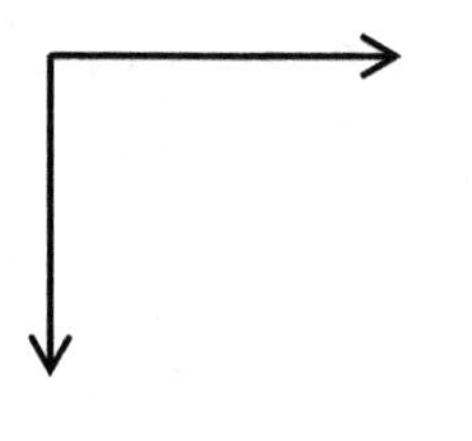

ladybiral

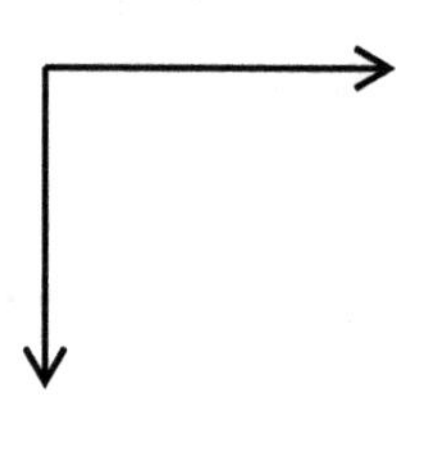

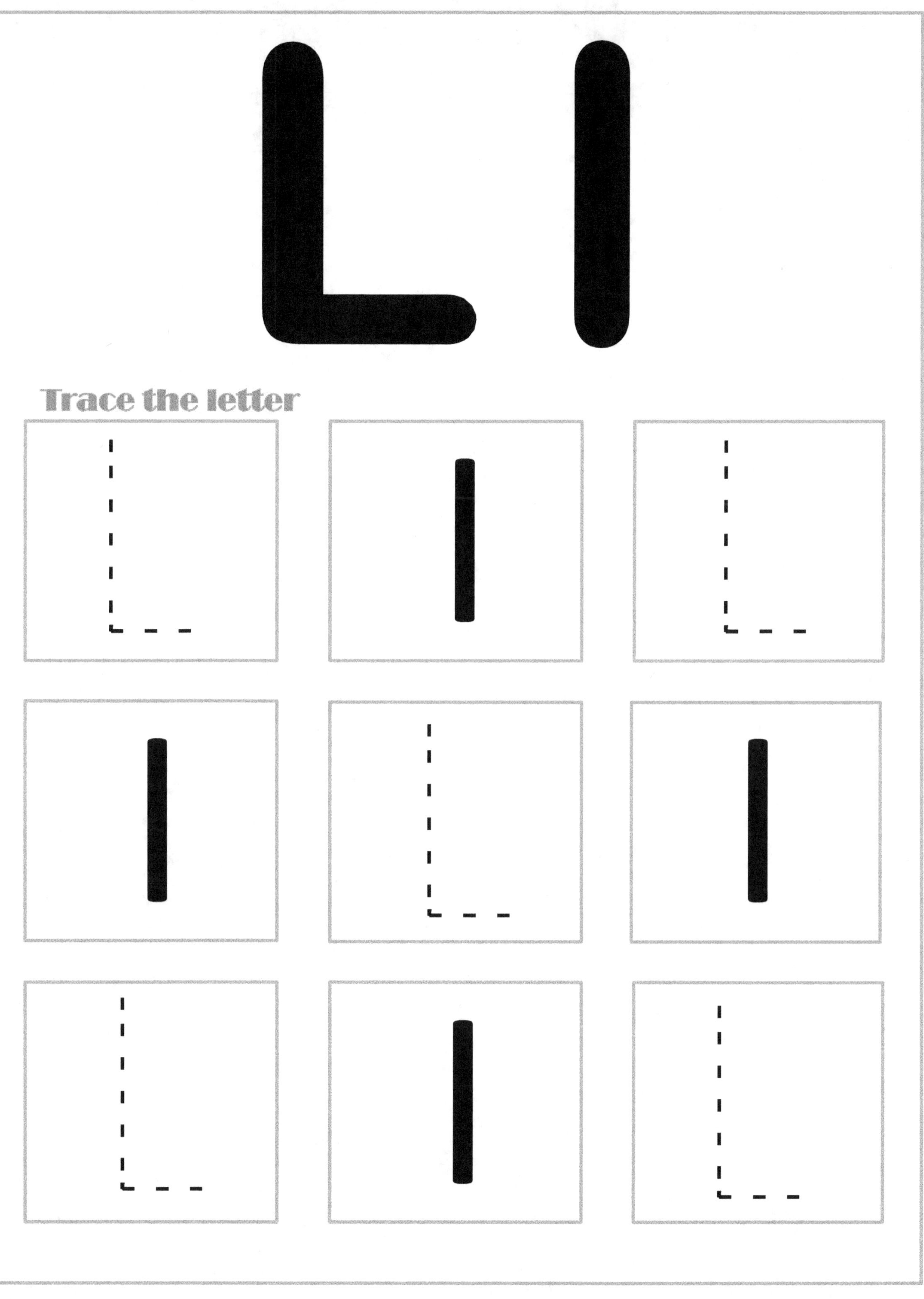
Trace the letter

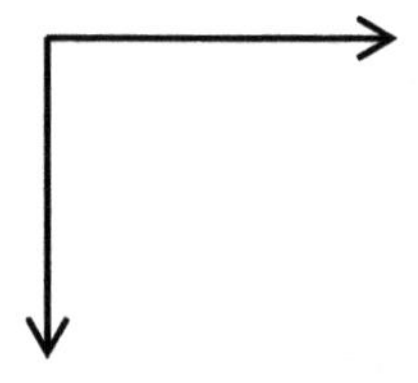

monkey

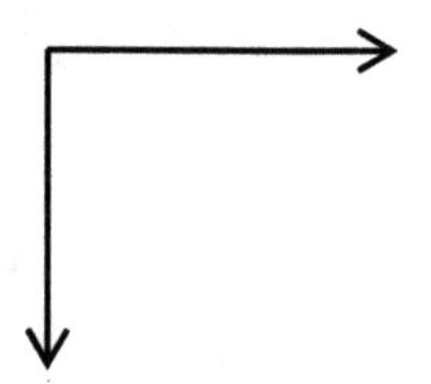

Mm

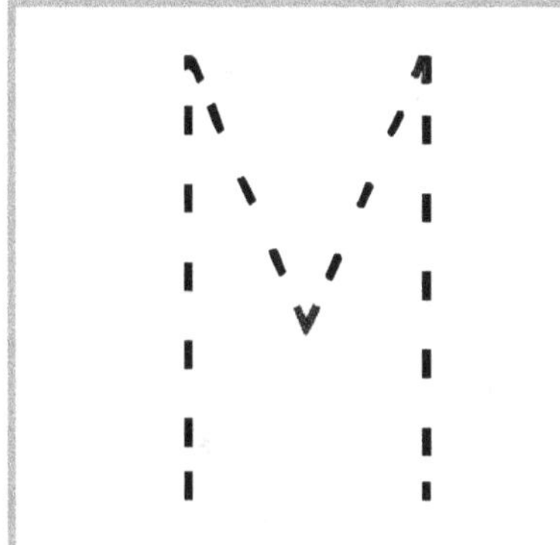

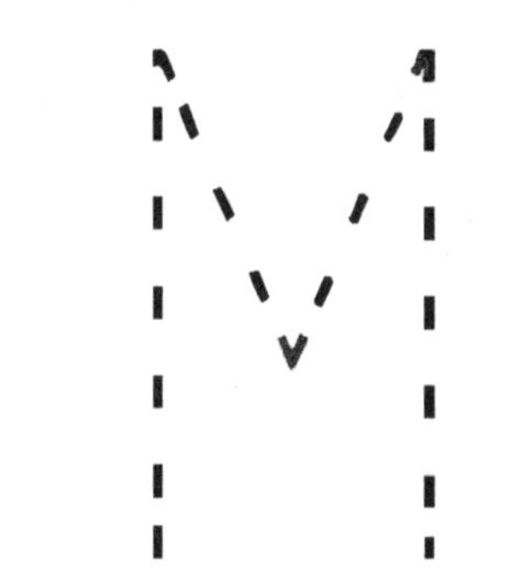
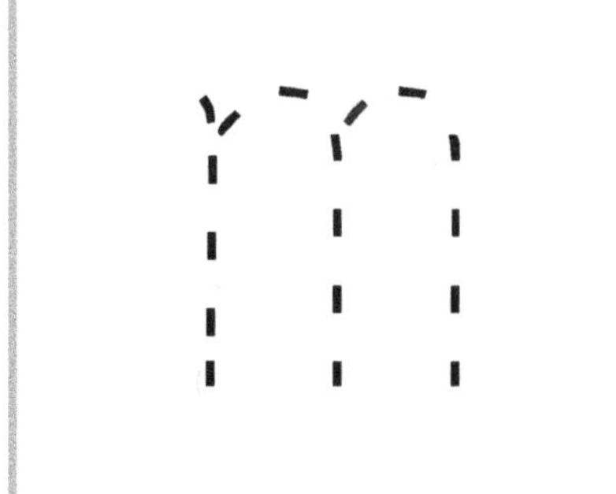

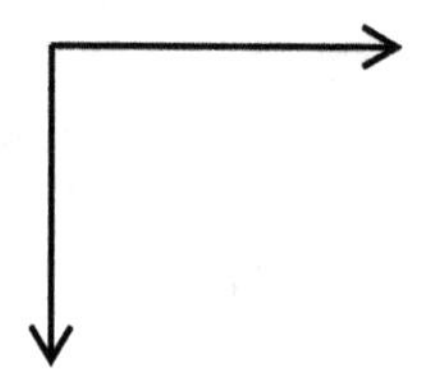

narwhal

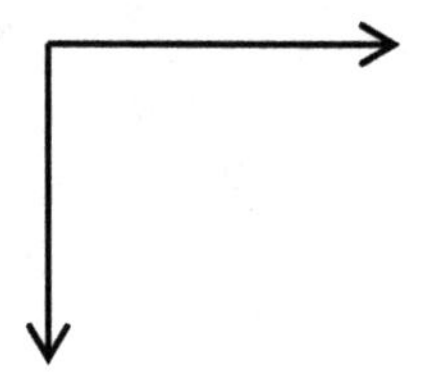

N n

Trace the letter

 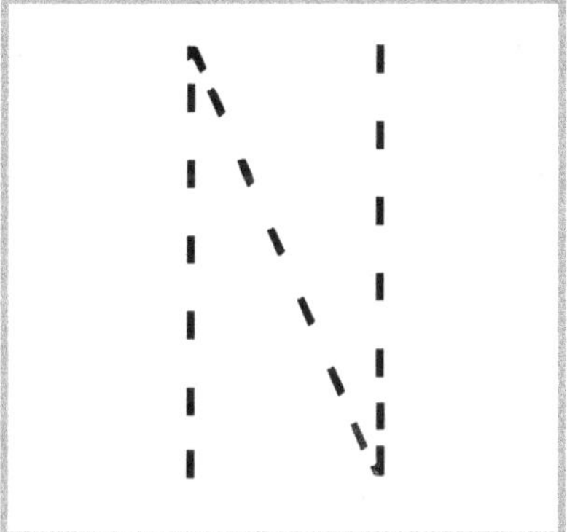

 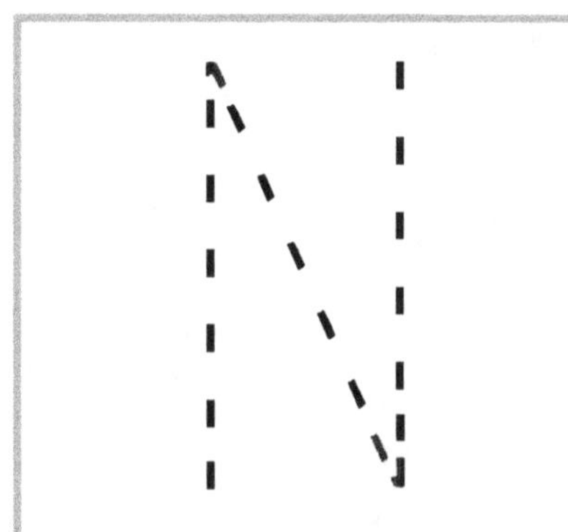 

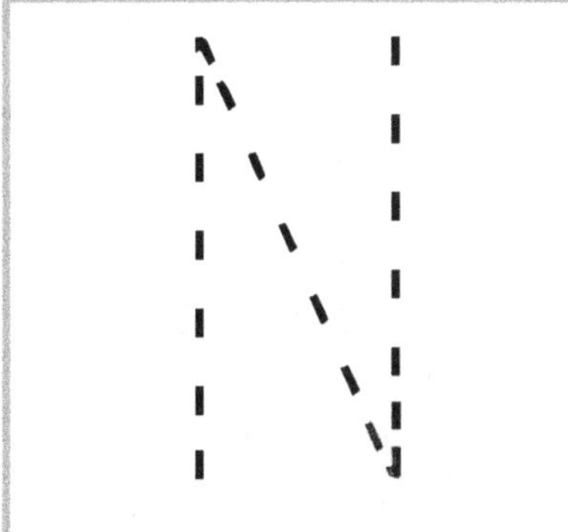 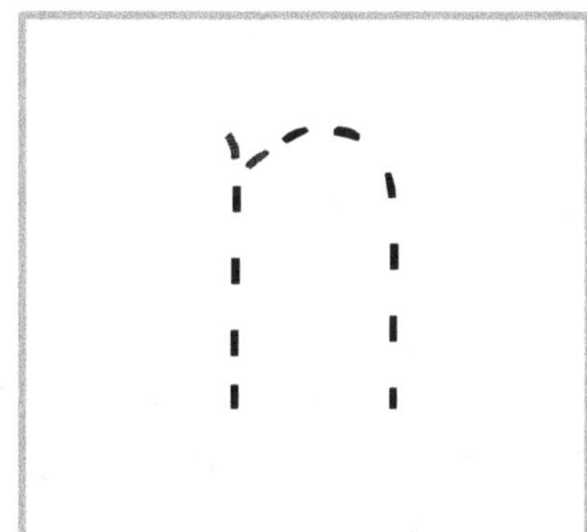

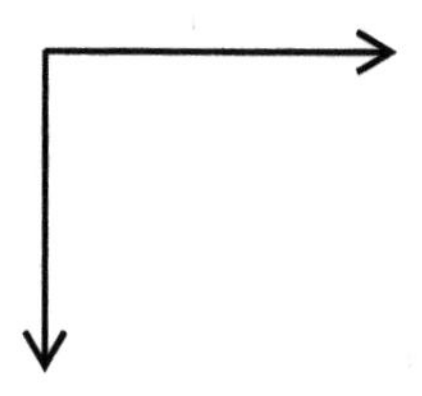

owl

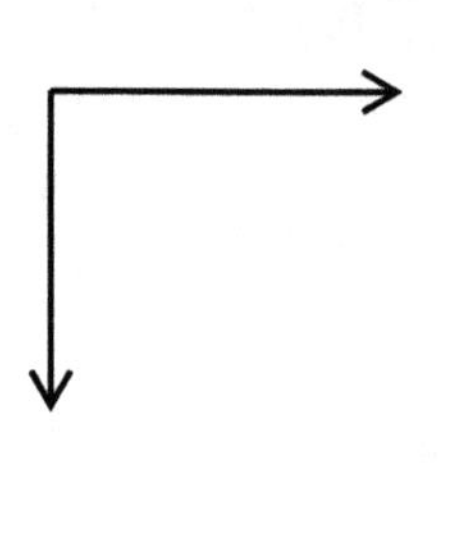

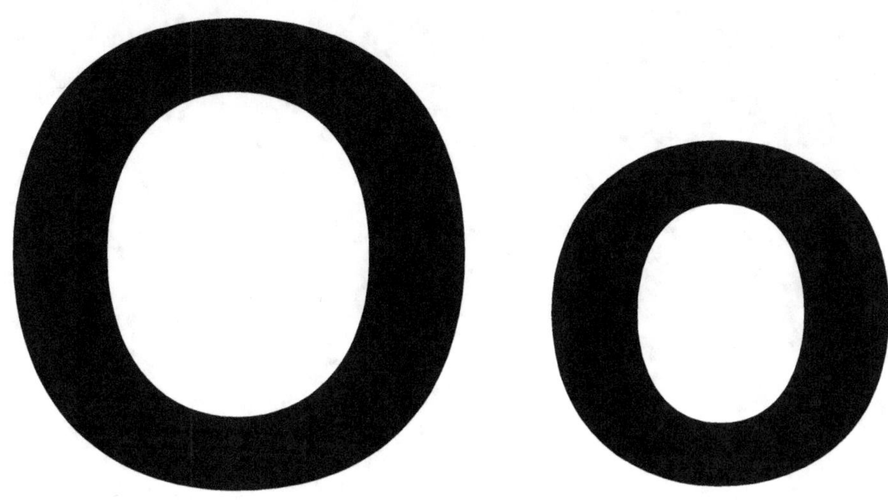

Trace the letter

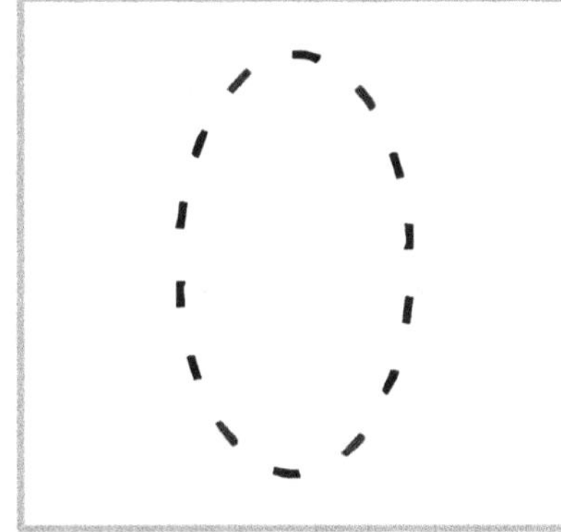

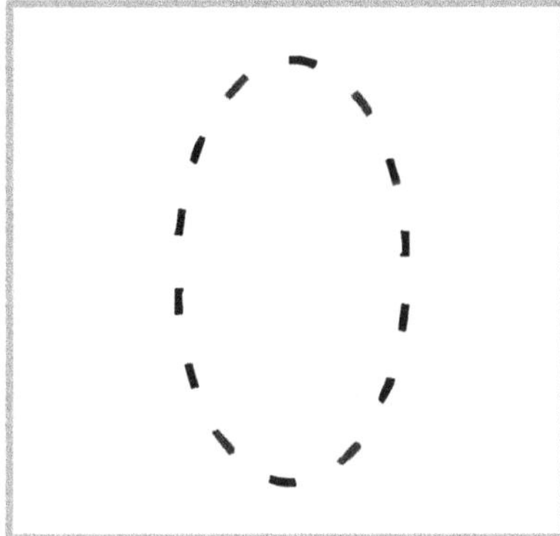

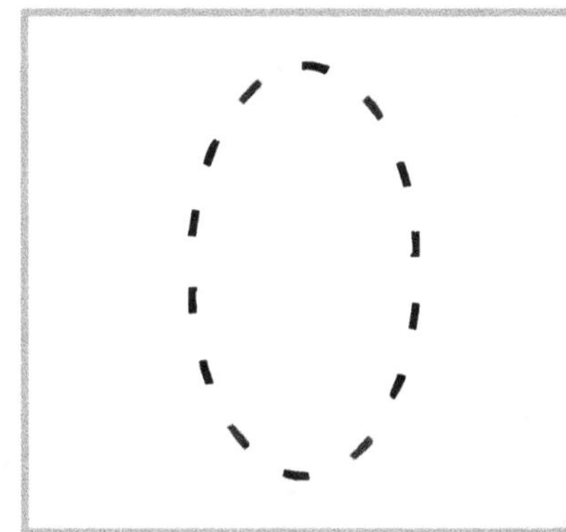

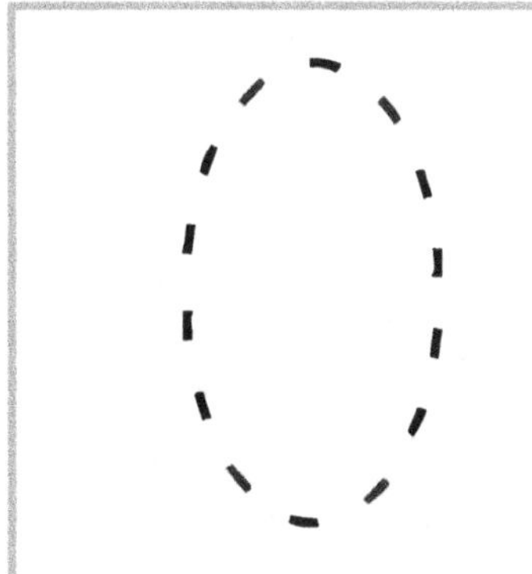

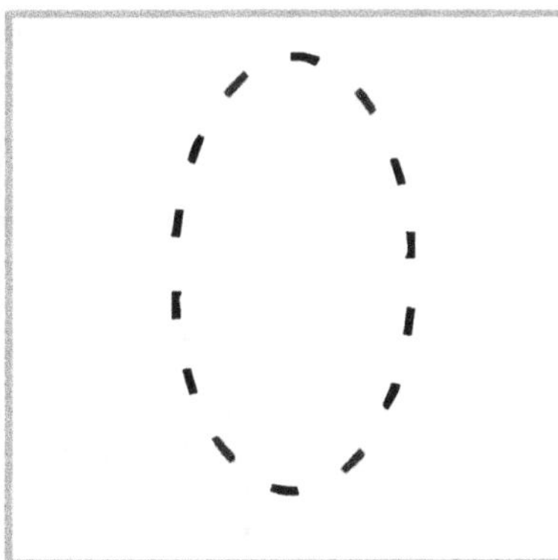

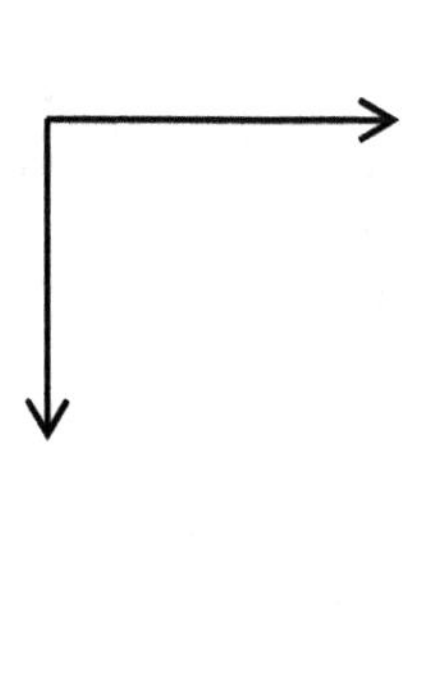

pig

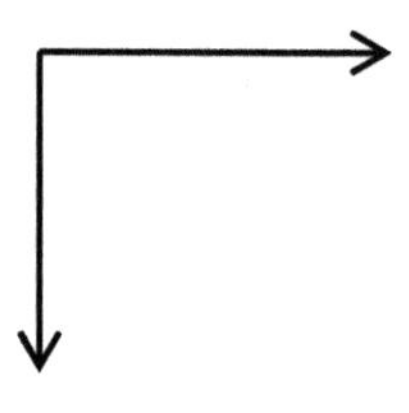

P p

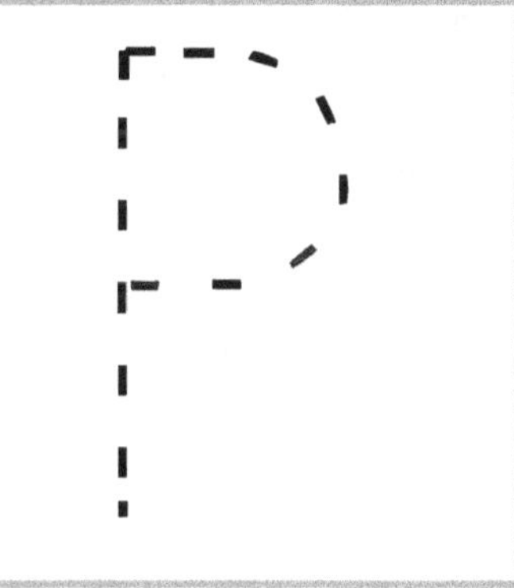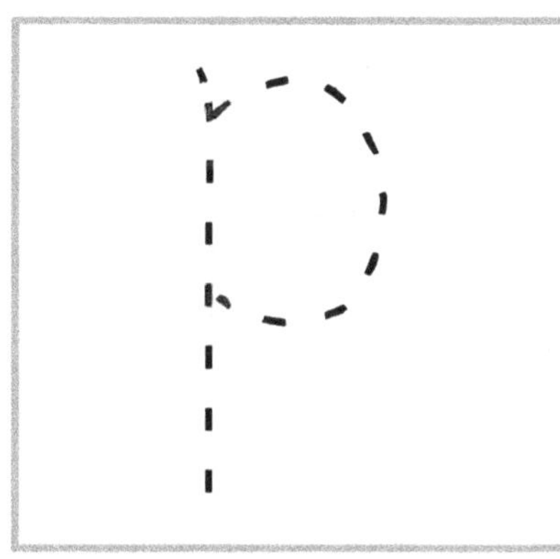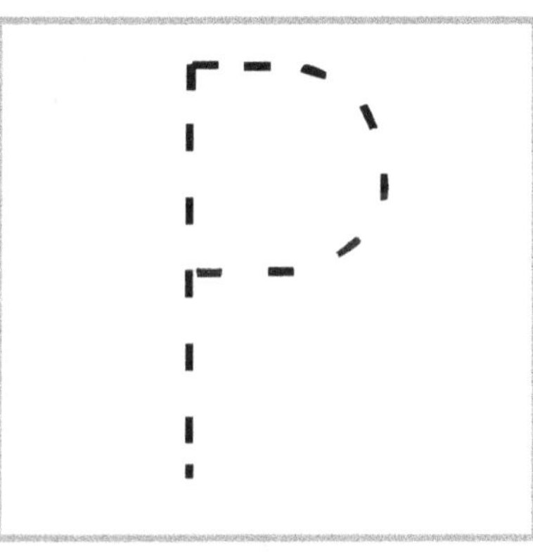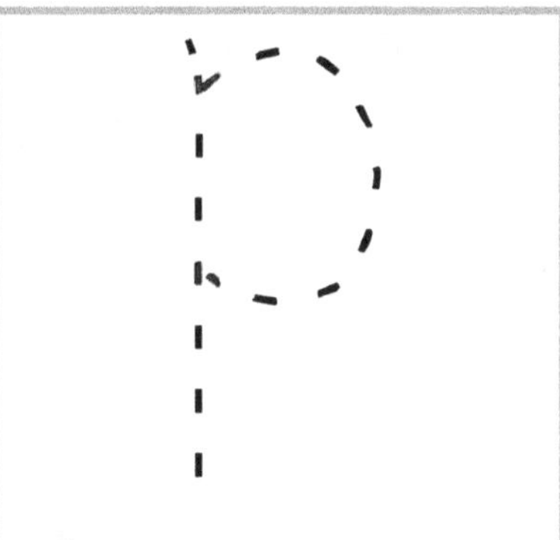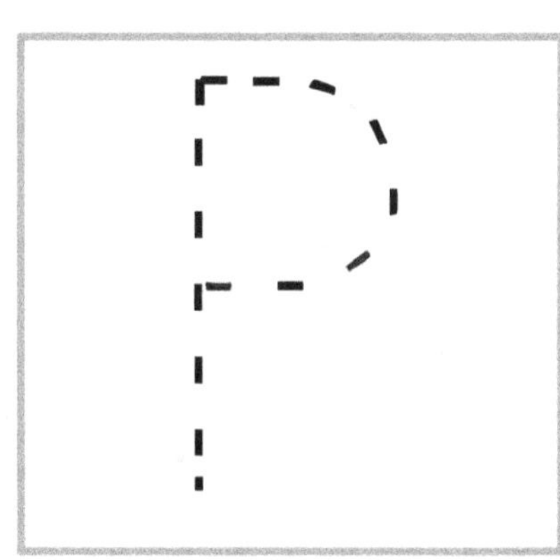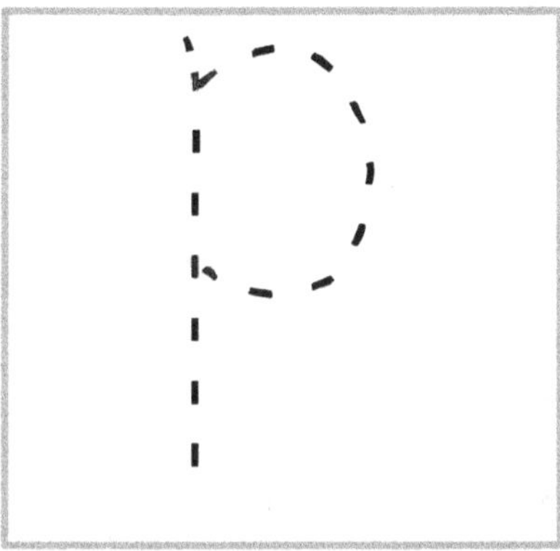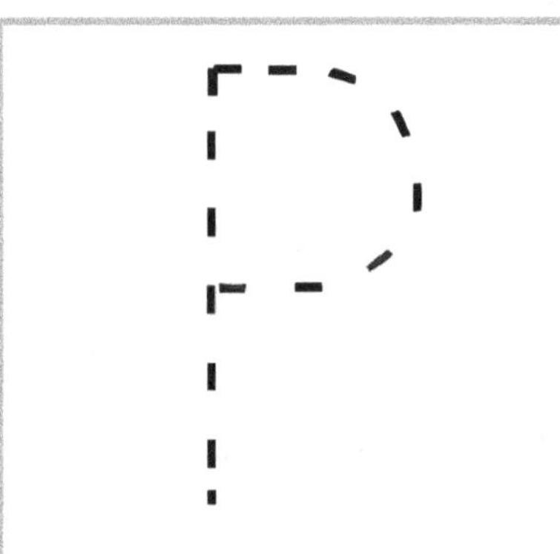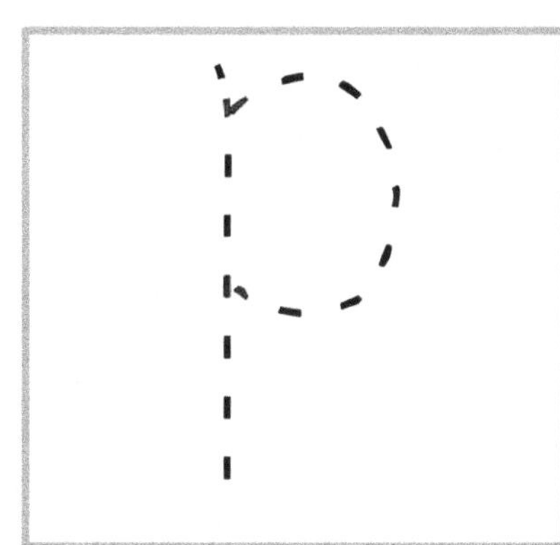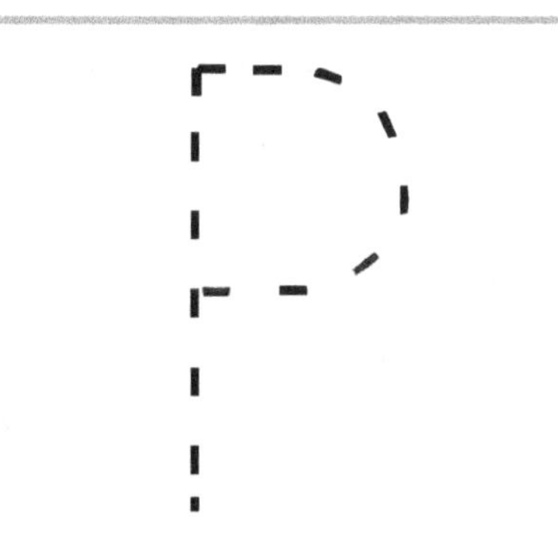

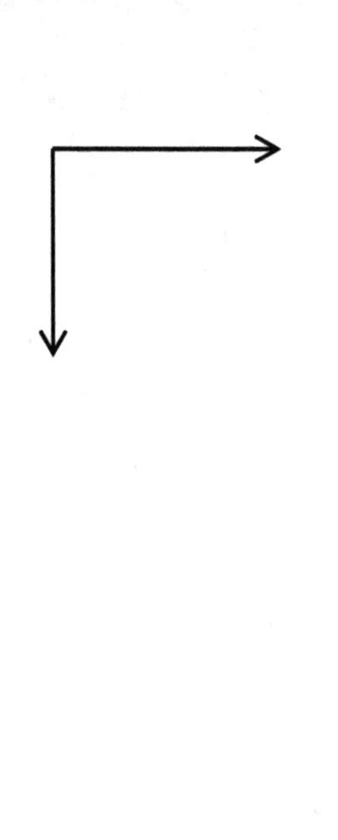

quail

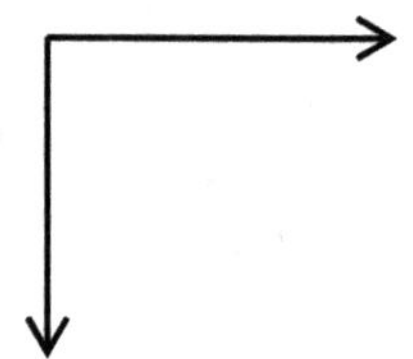

Trace the letter

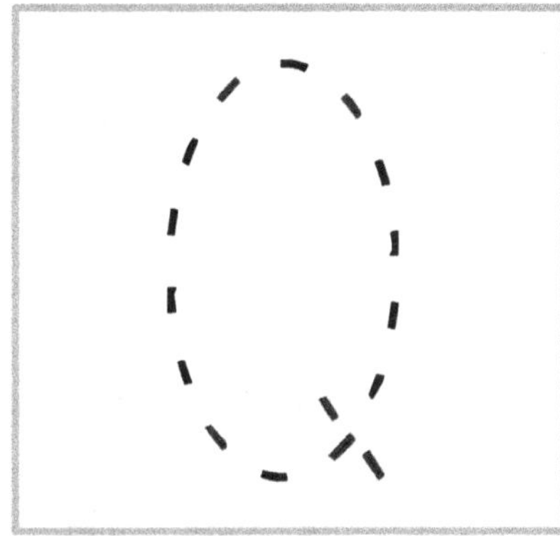
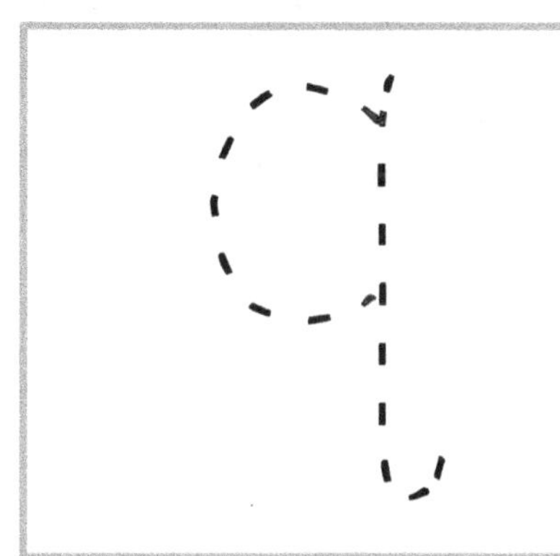
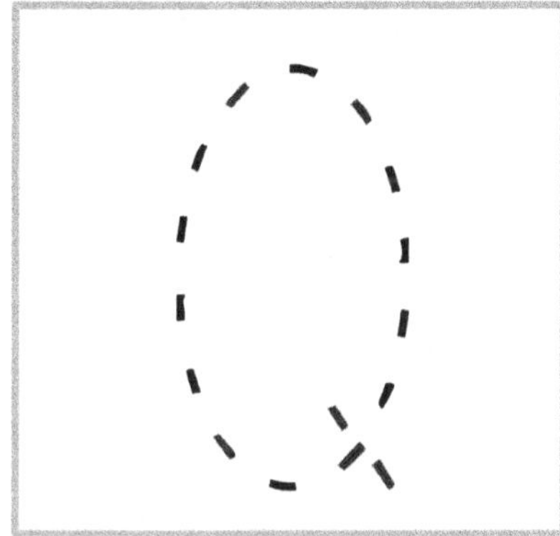

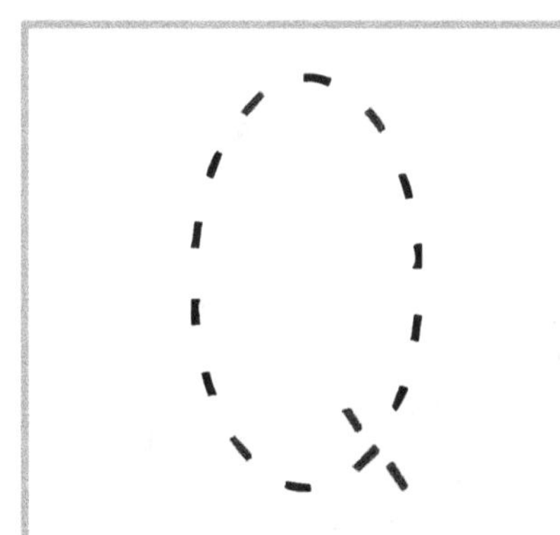
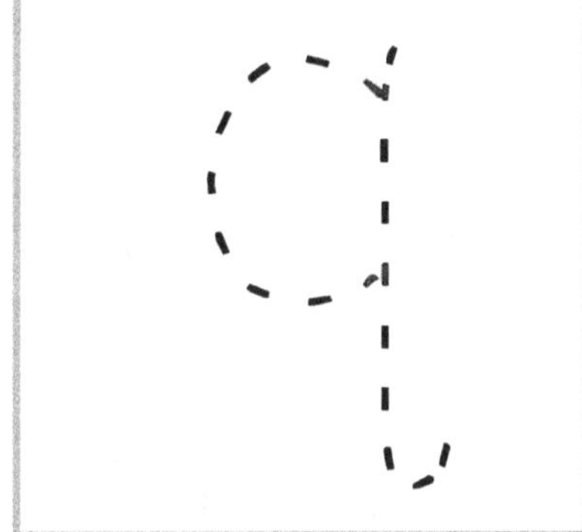
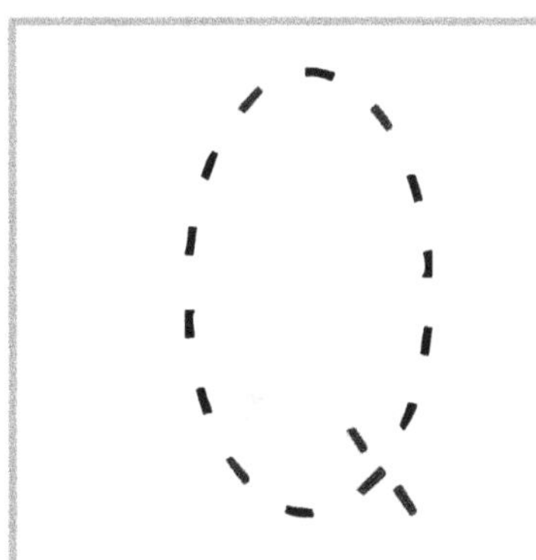
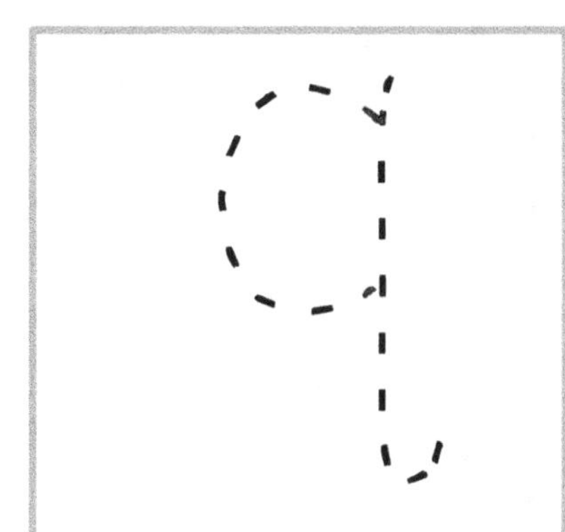
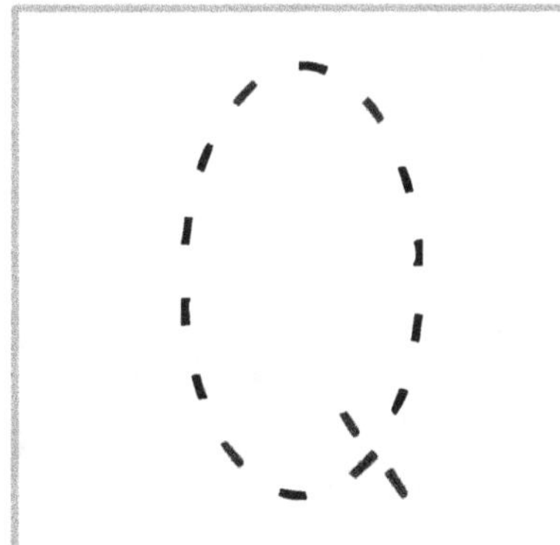

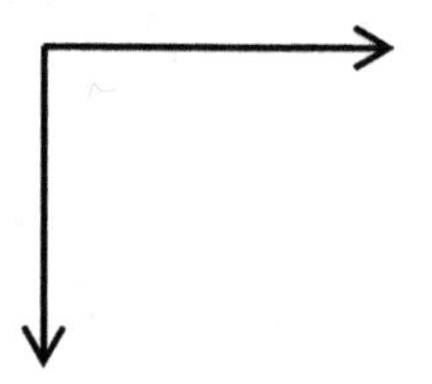

rat

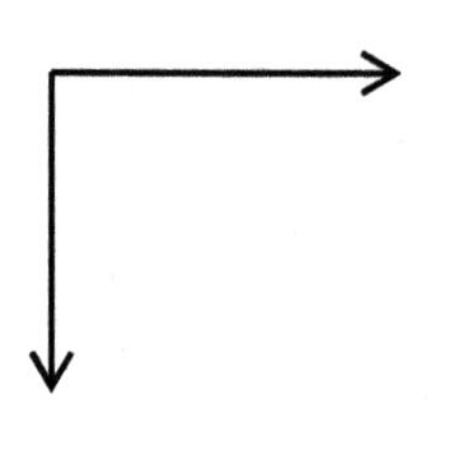

R r

Trace the letter

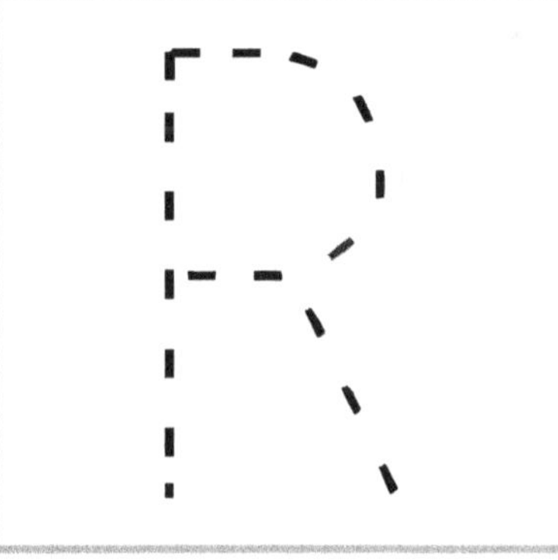
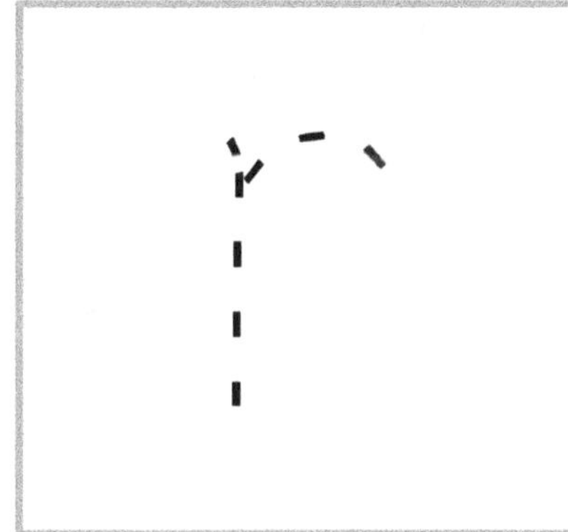
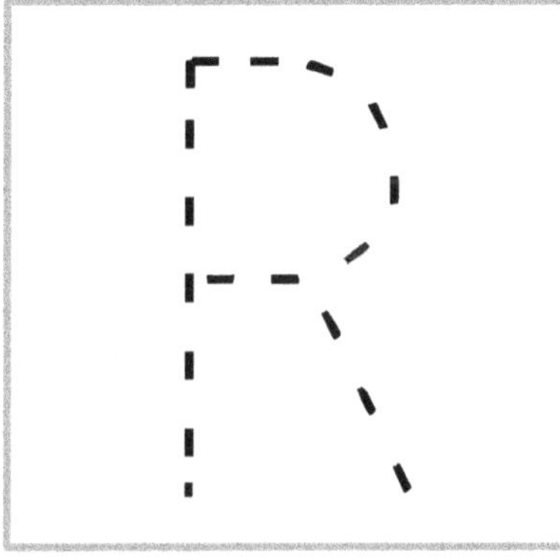

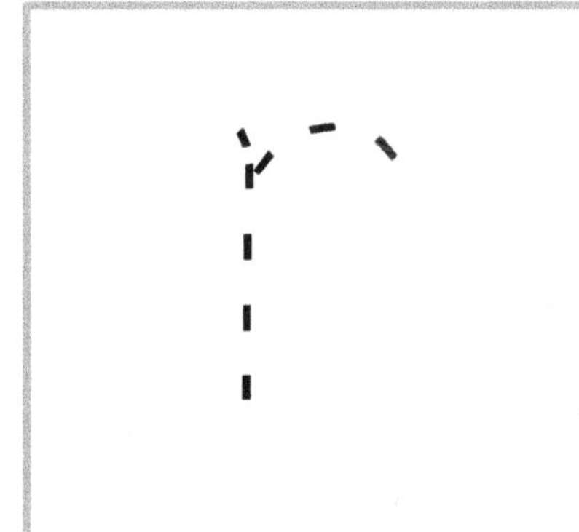

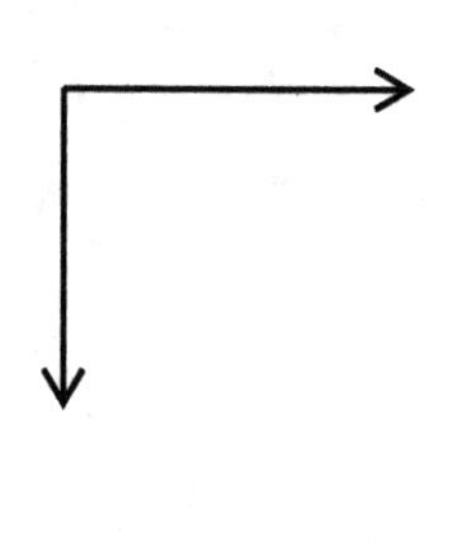

seal

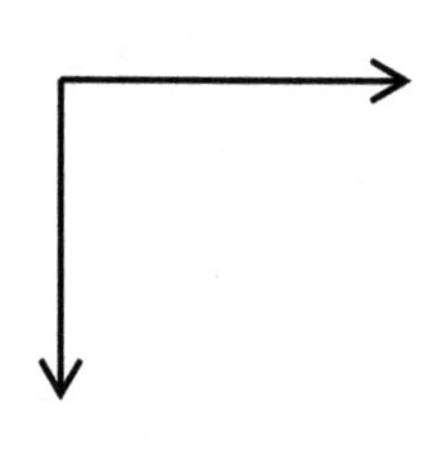

Ss

Trace the letter

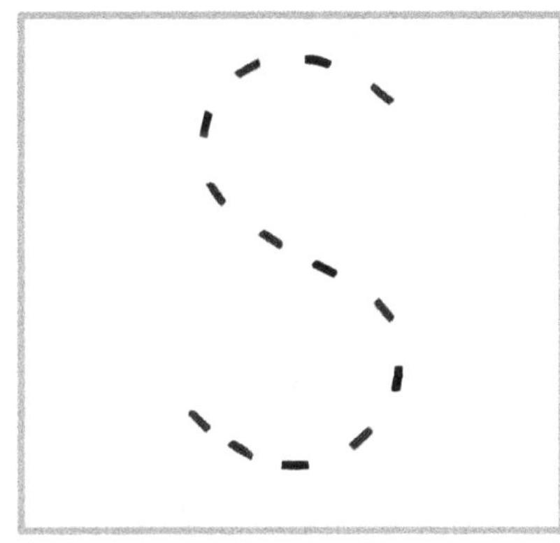 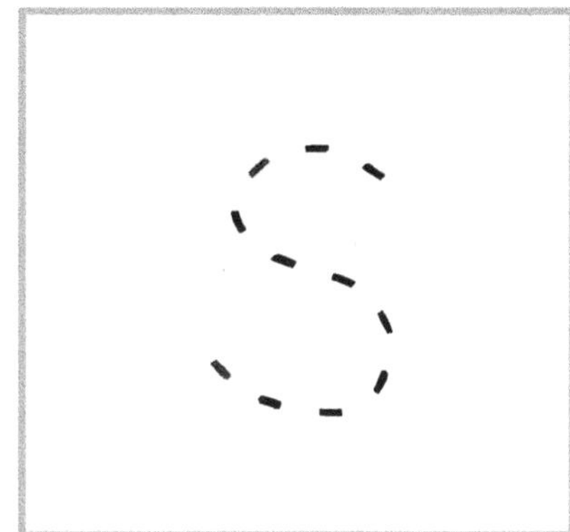 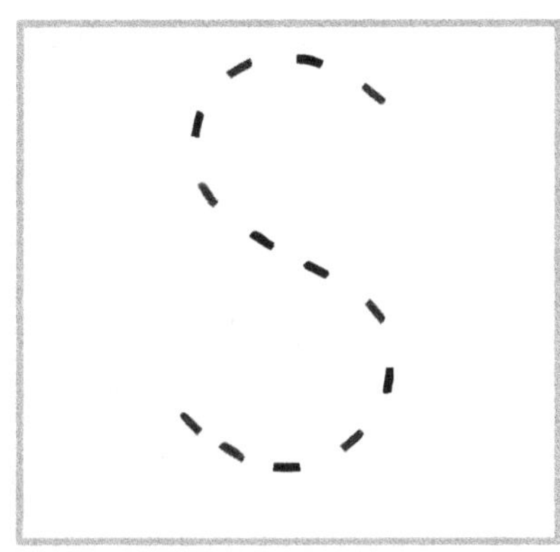

 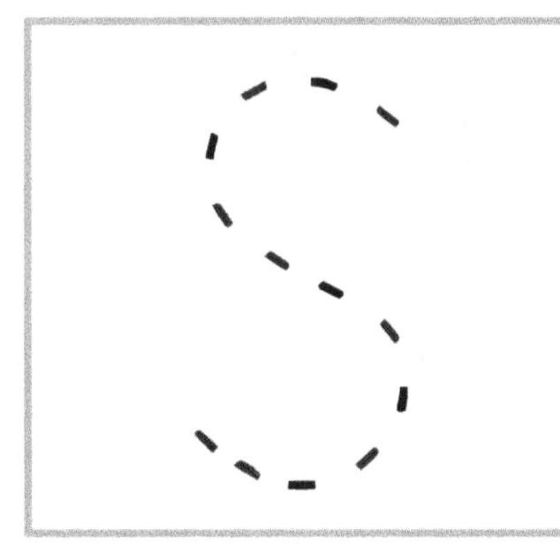 

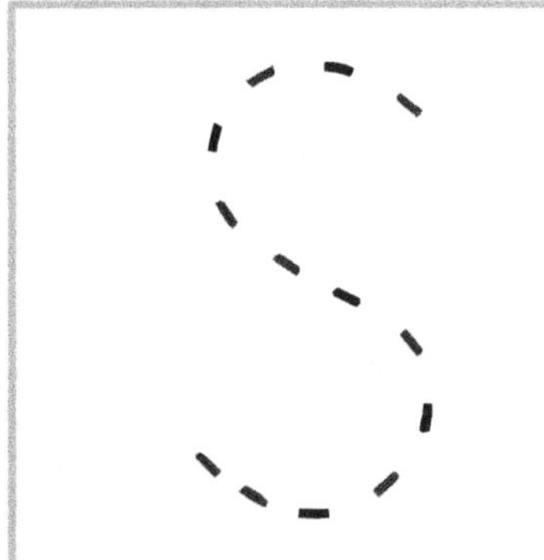  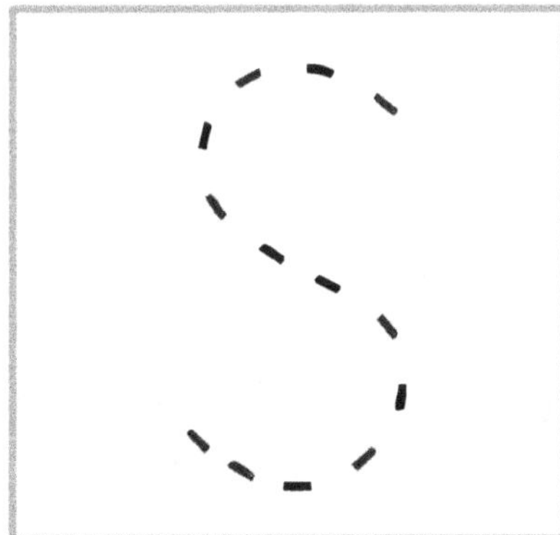

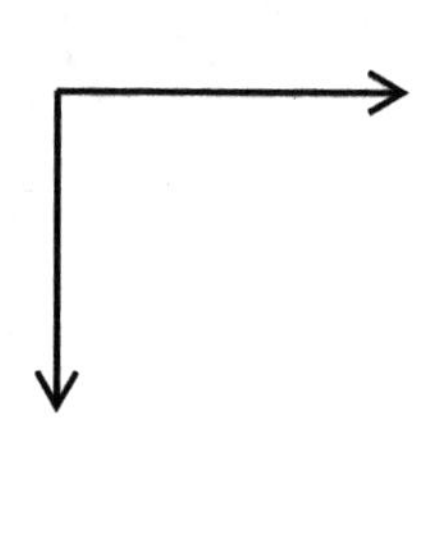

turtle

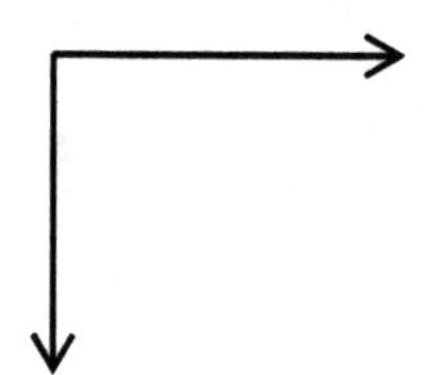

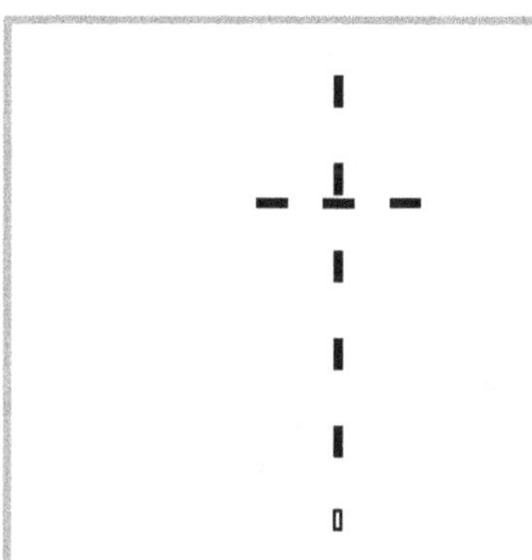

Trace the letter

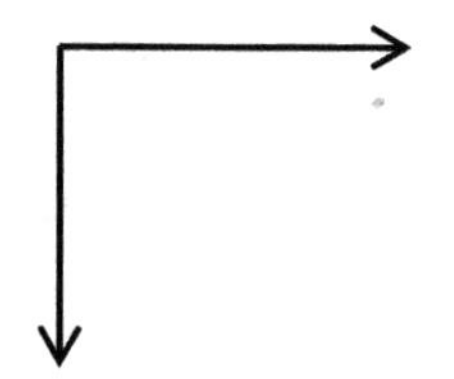

unicorn

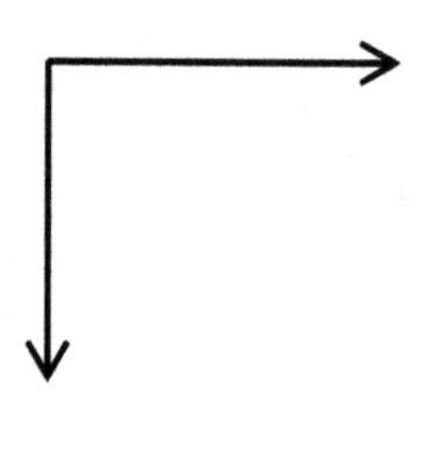

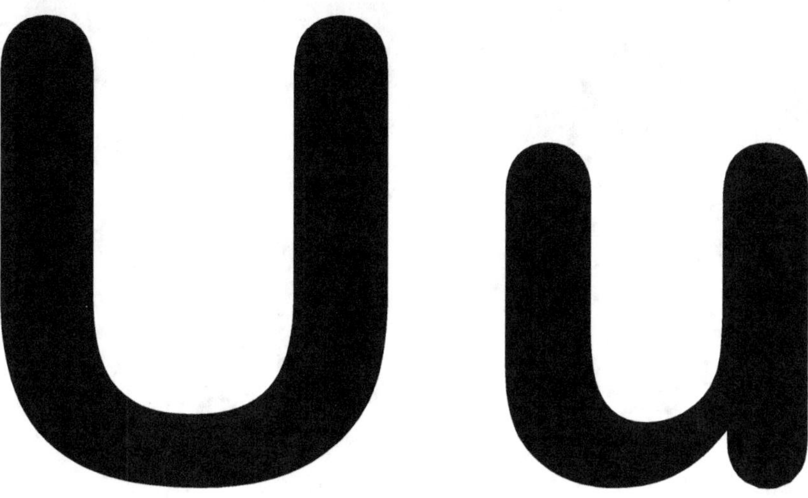

Trace the letter

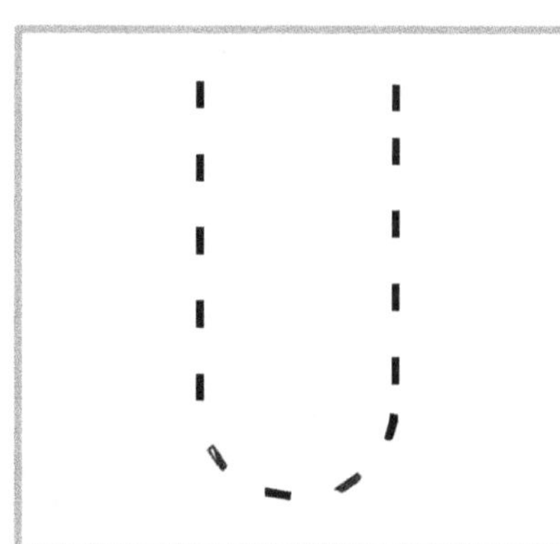

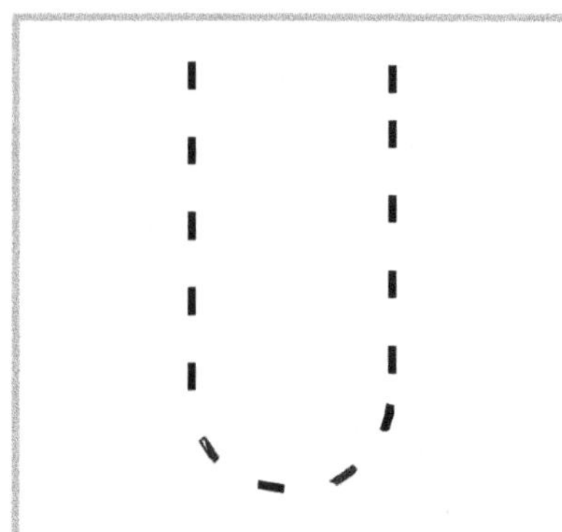

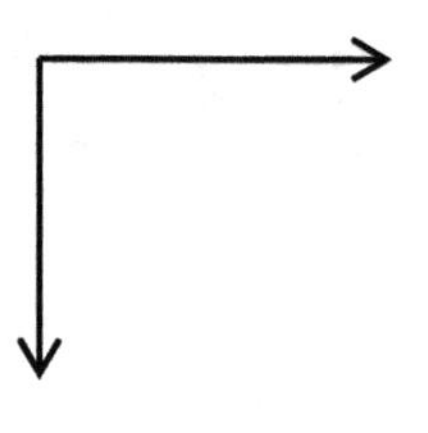

vulture

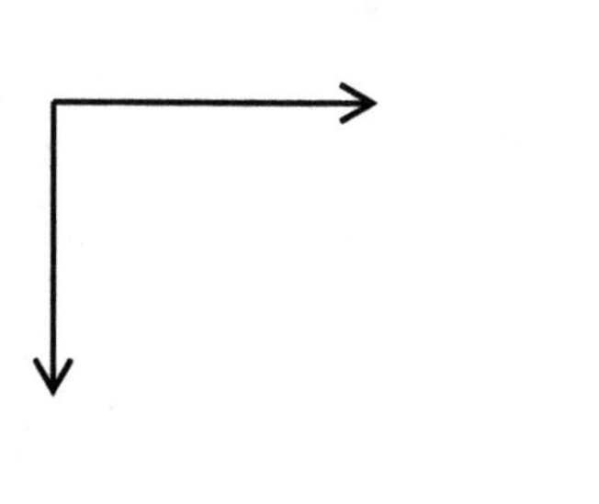

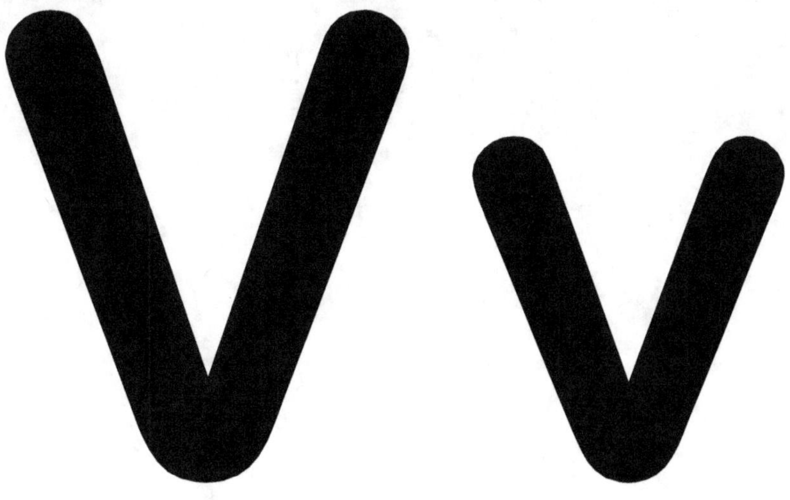

Trace the letter

 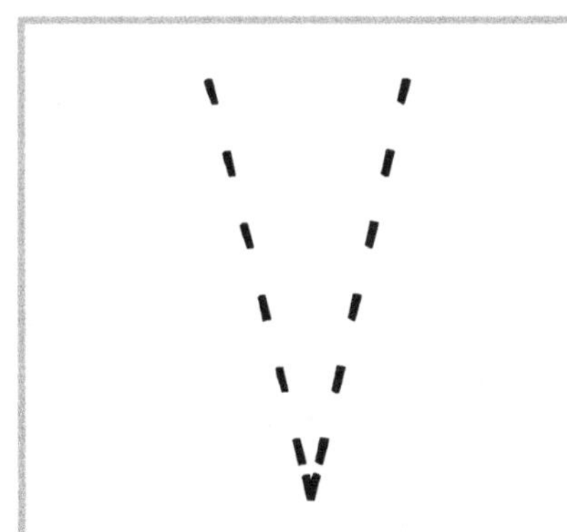 

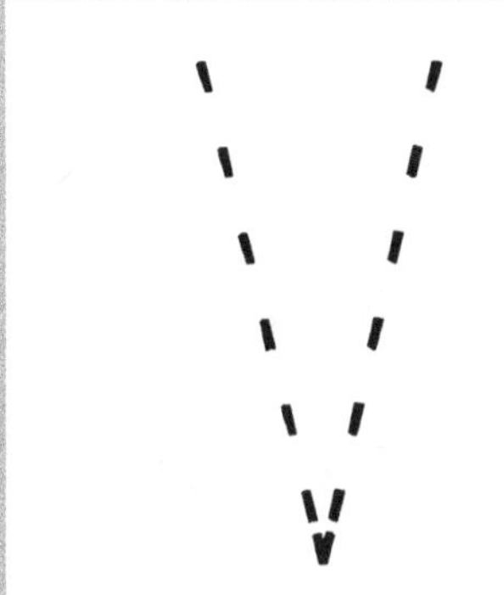  

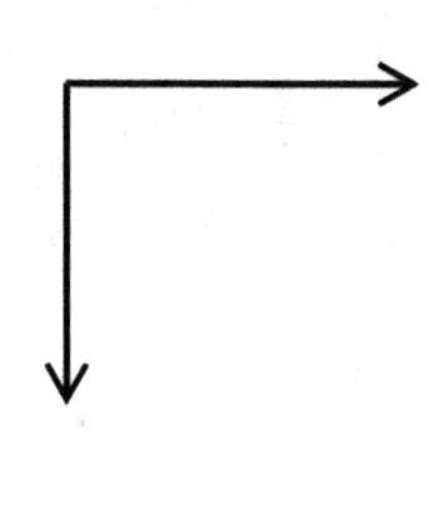

wolf

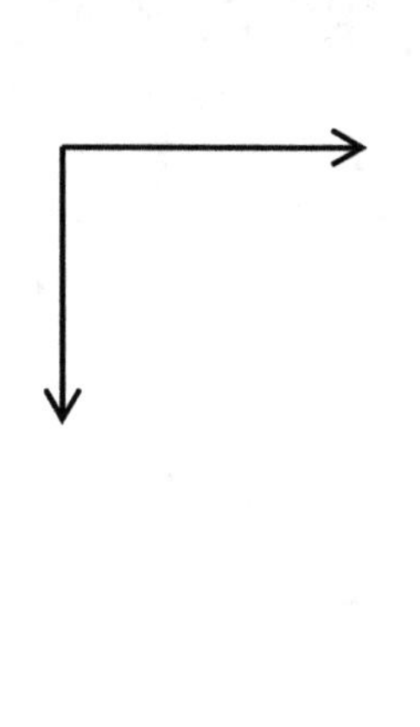

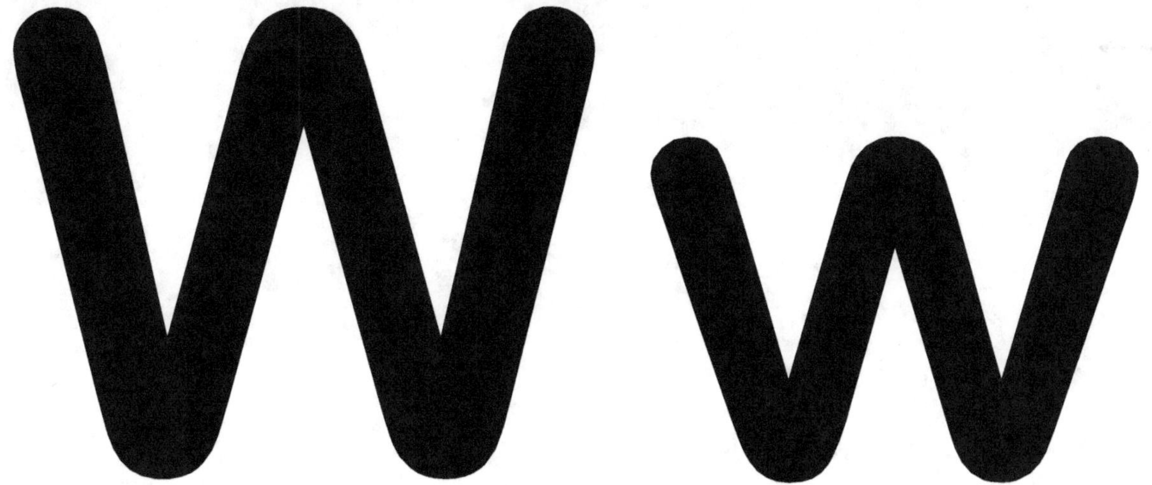

Trace the letter

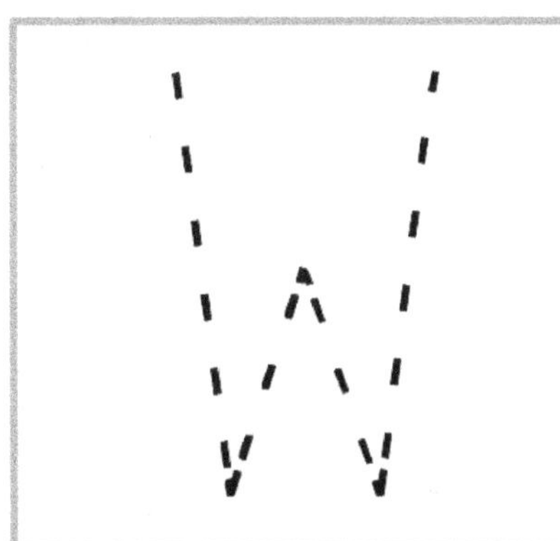

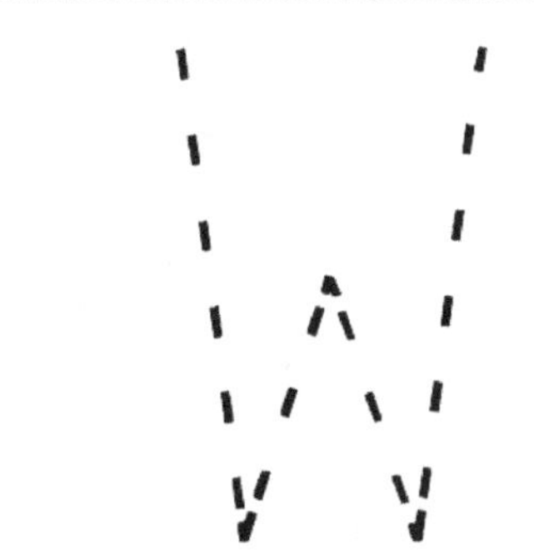

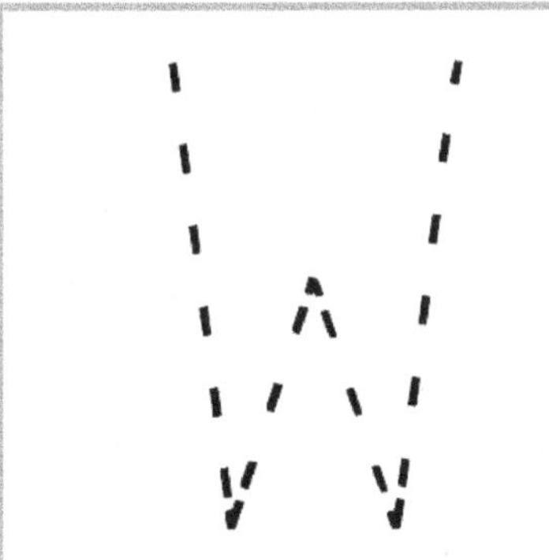

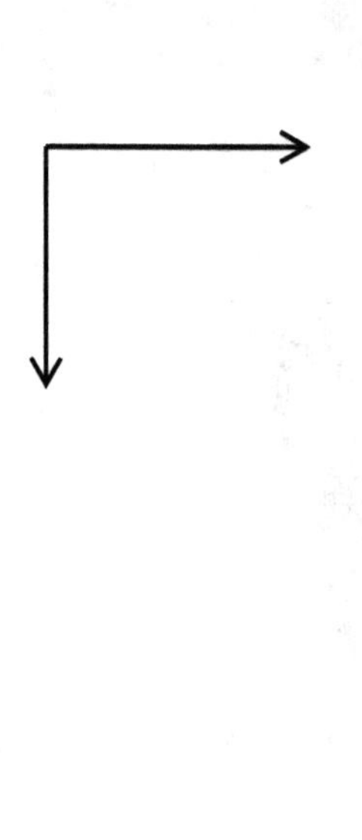

yabby

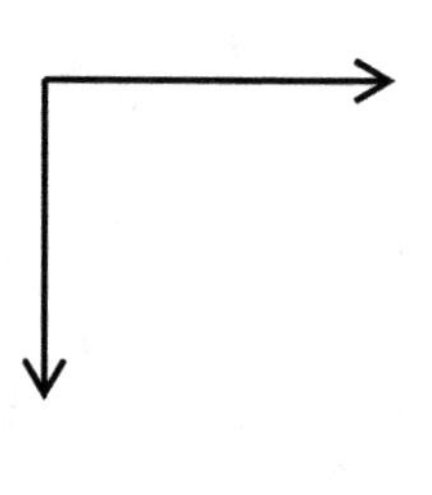

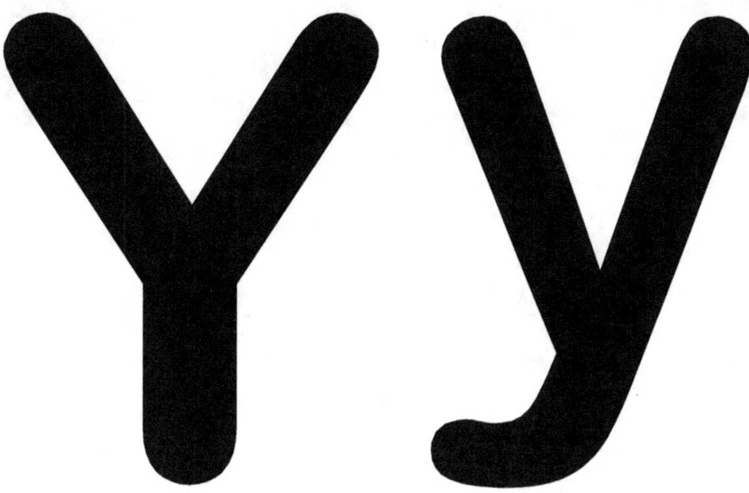

Trace the letter

 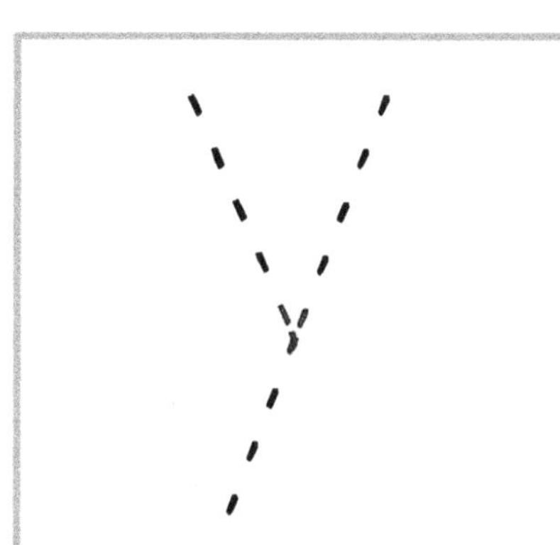 

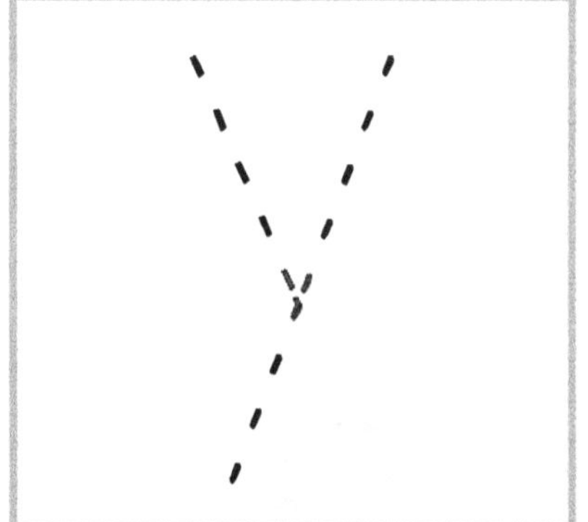 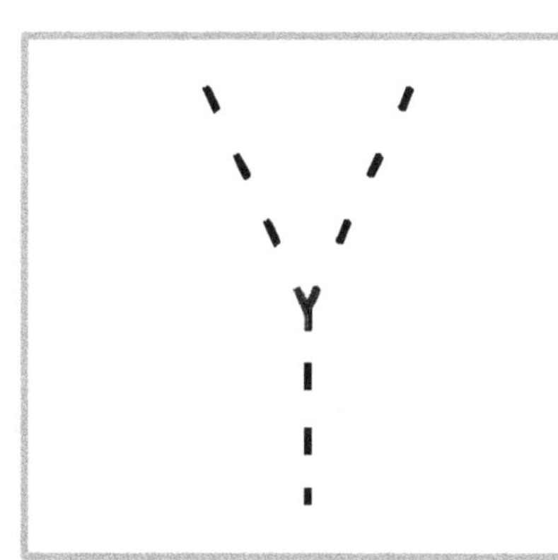 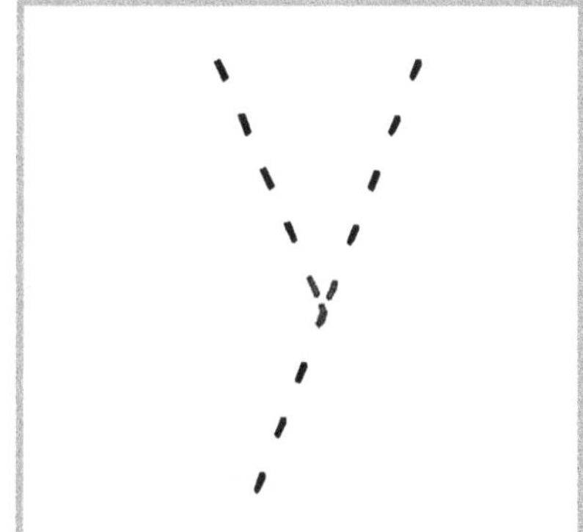

 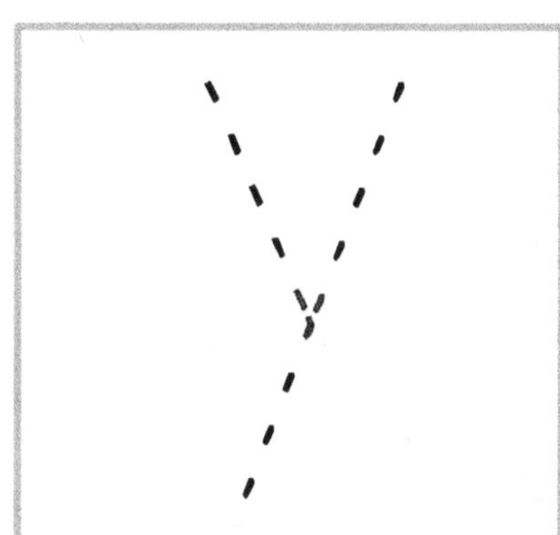 

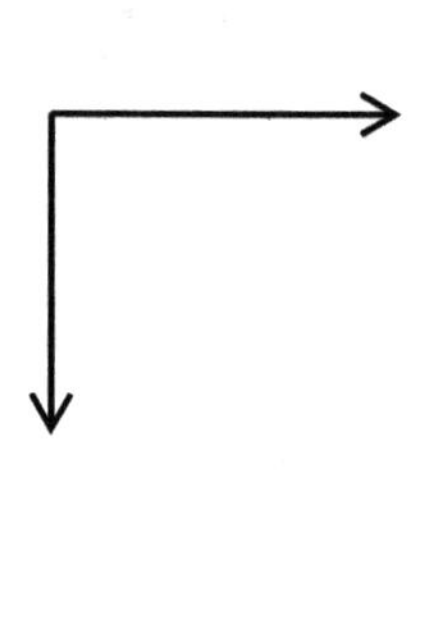

zebra

More small animals

dog

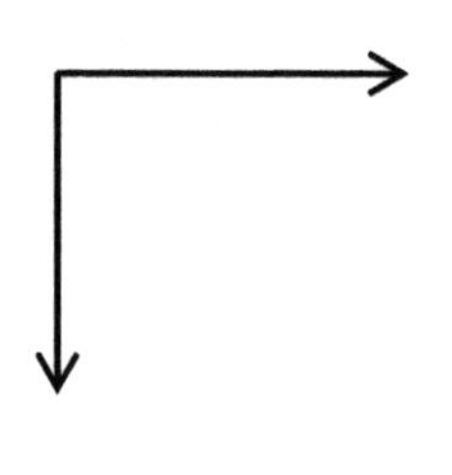

grasshopper

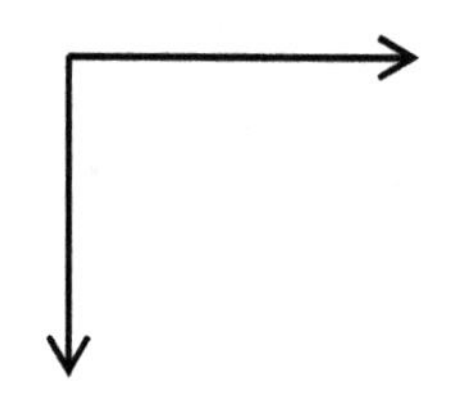

crab

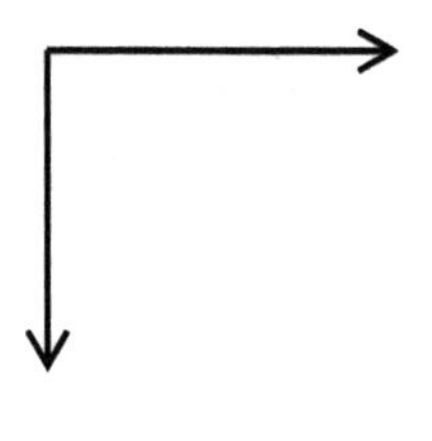

cat

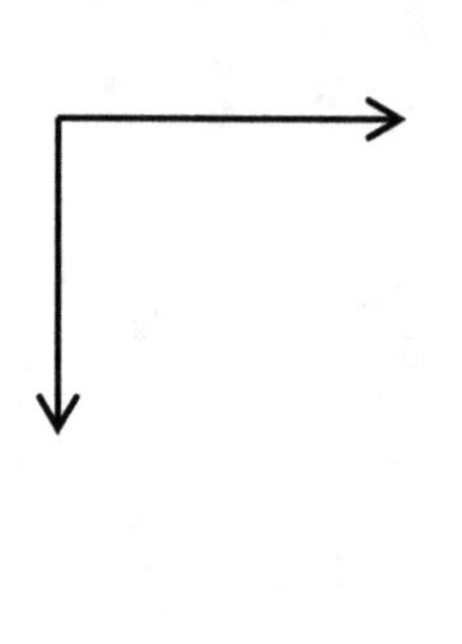

dodo

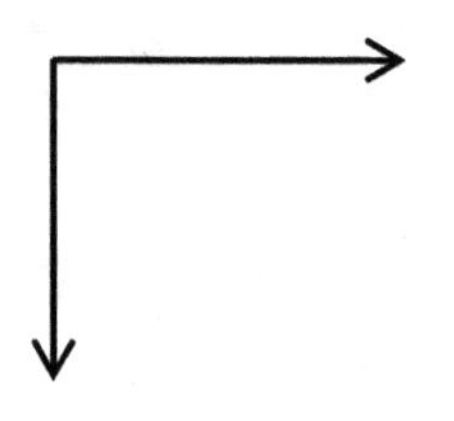

llama

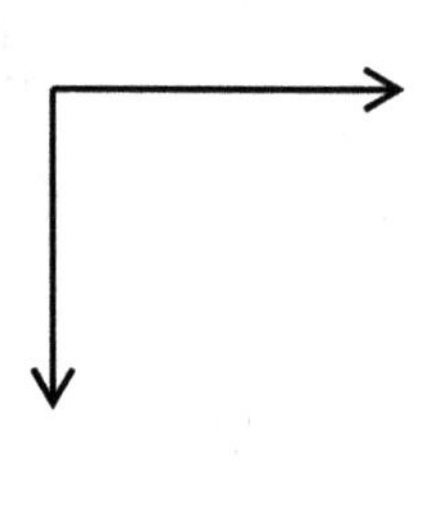

butterfly

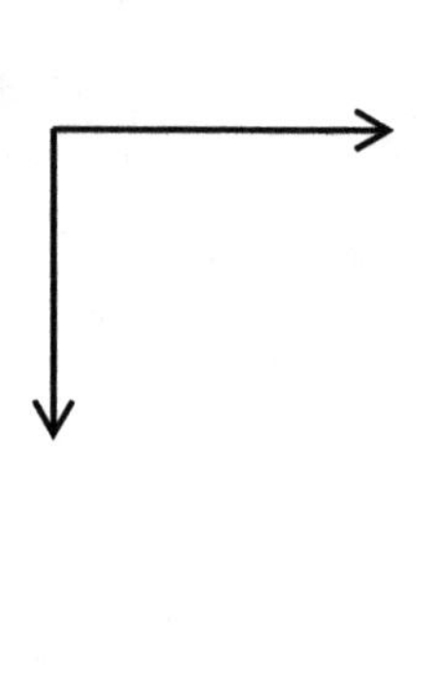

fish

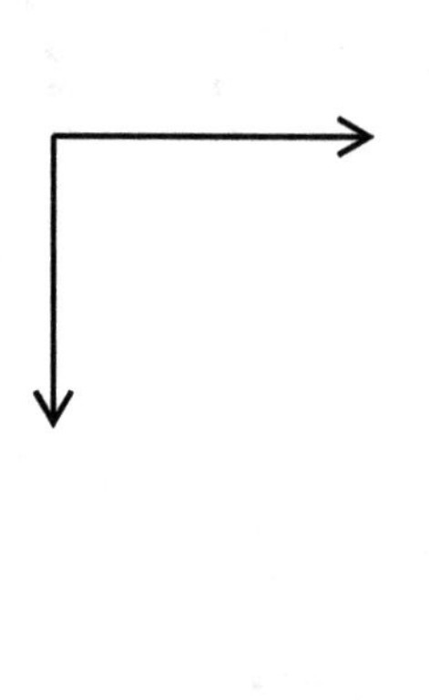

worm

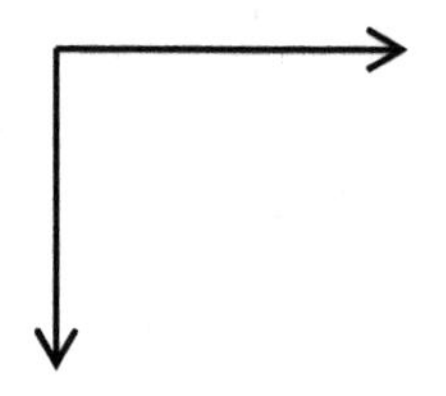

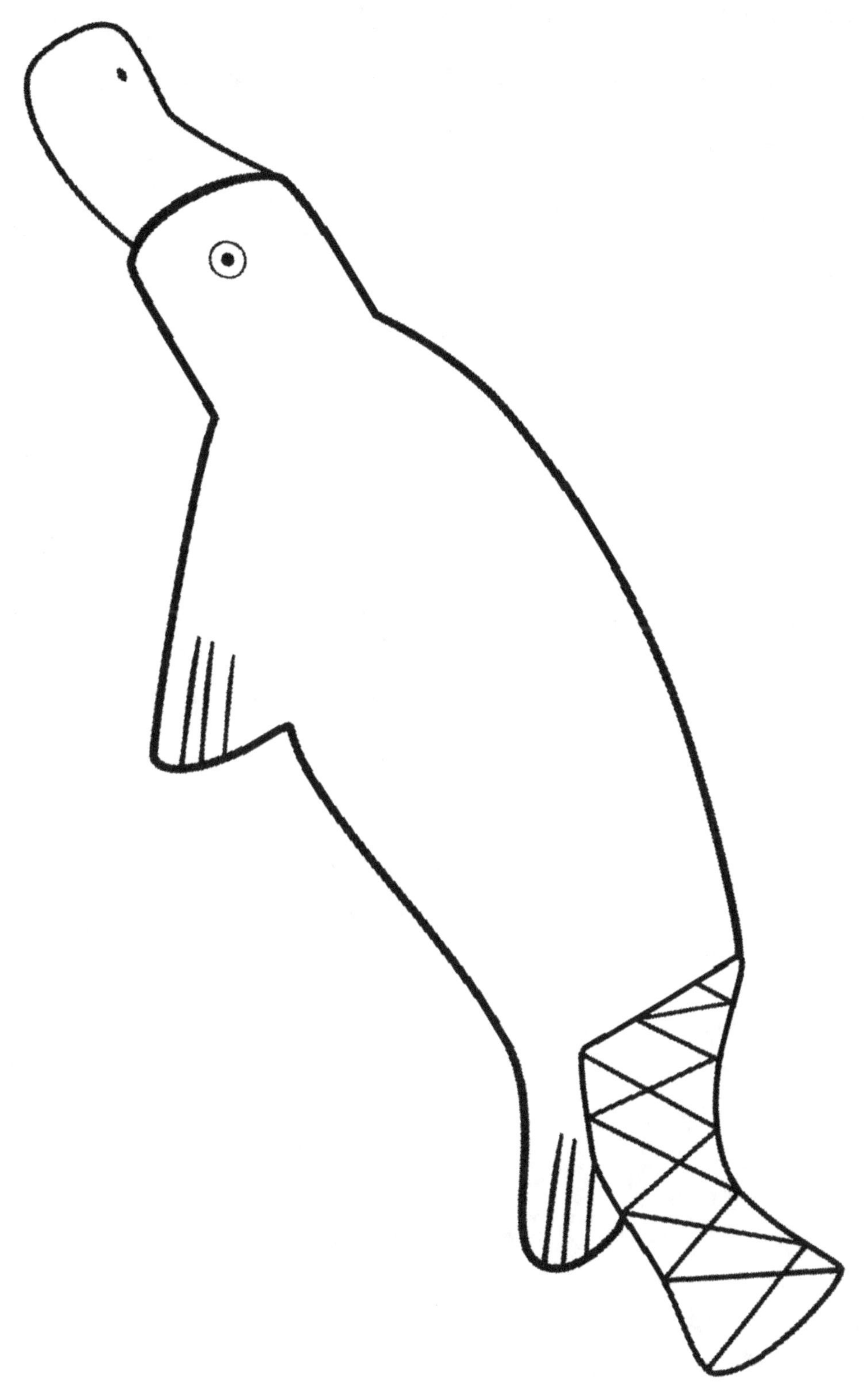

platypus

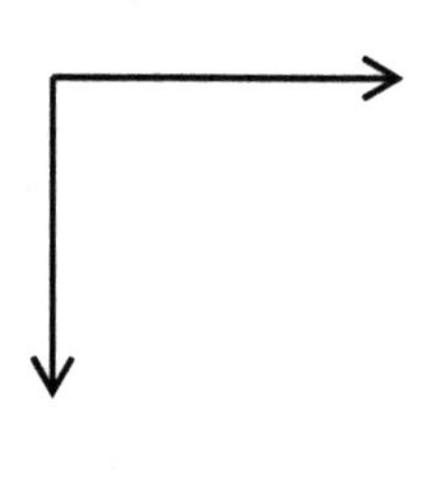

octopus

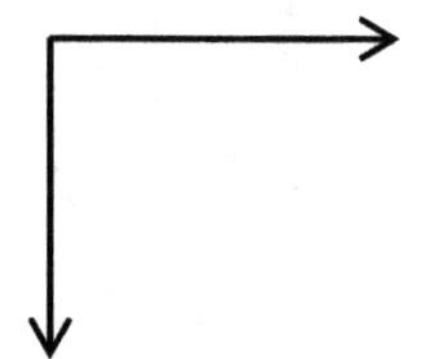

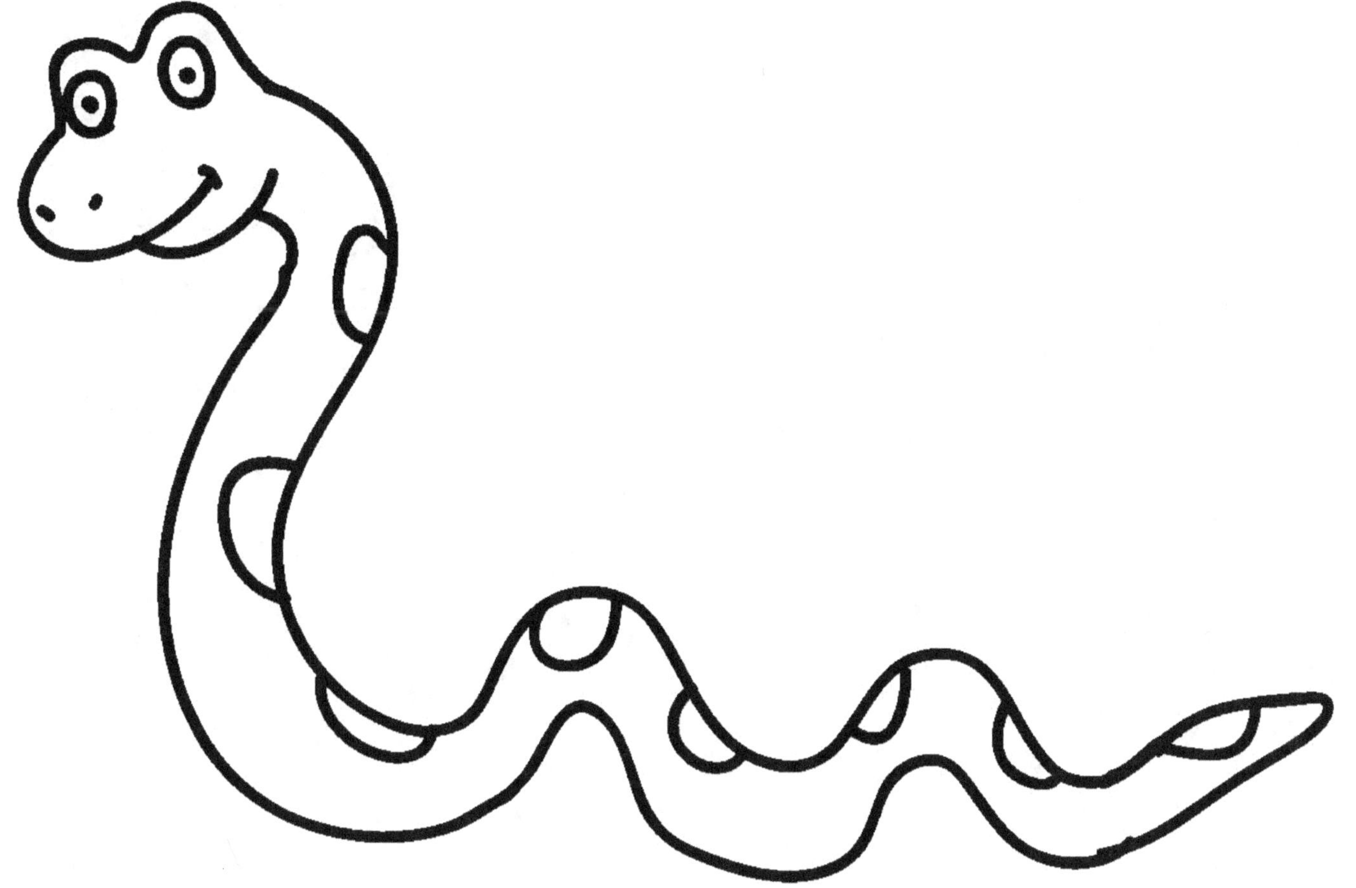

snake

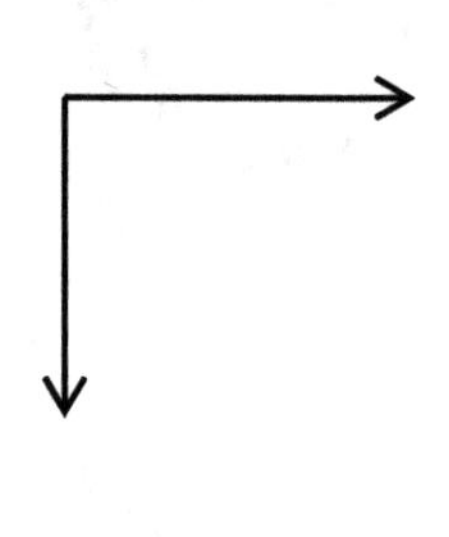

lamb

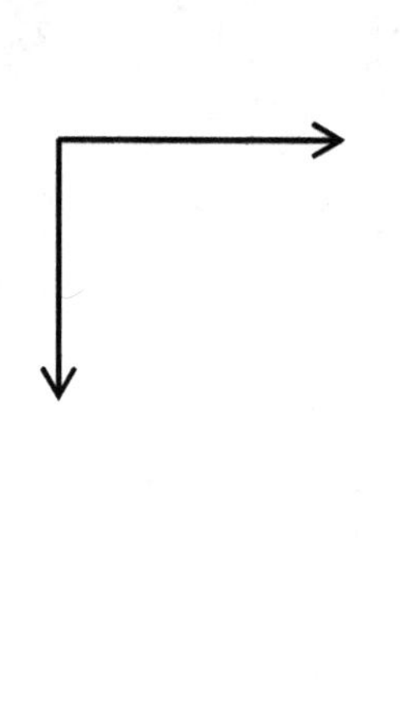

bear

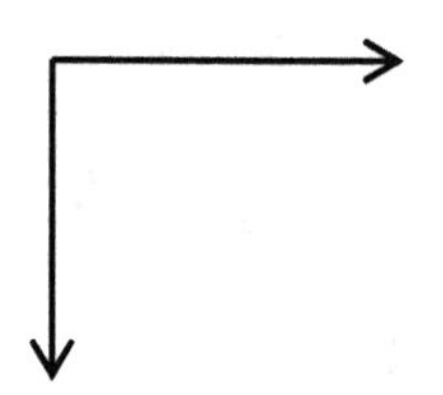

hippo

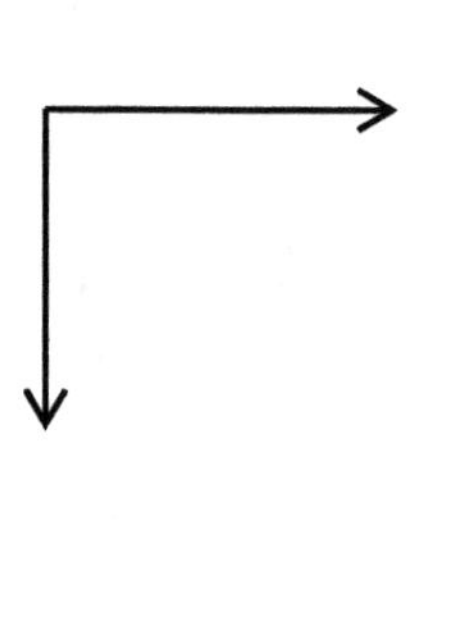

shark

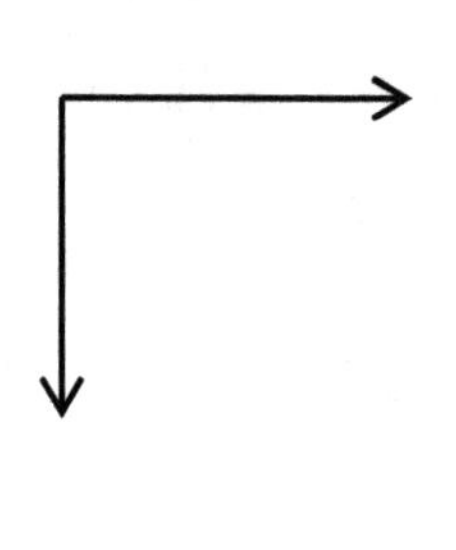

Color the animals in the picture

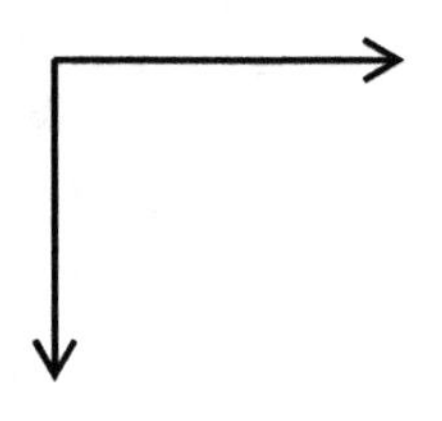

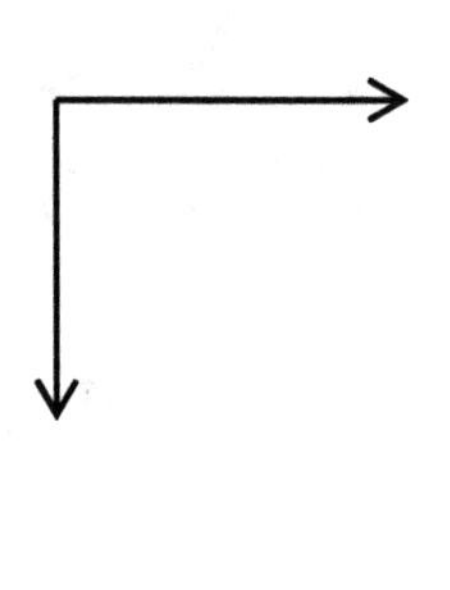

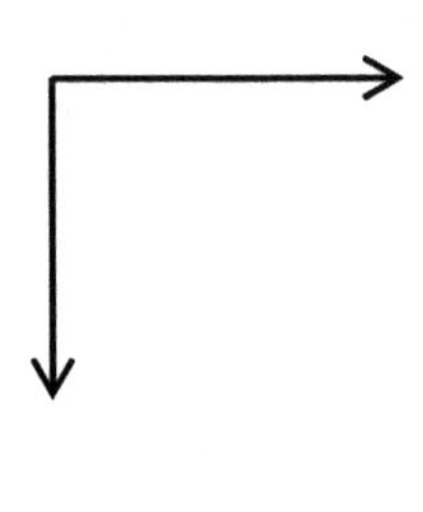

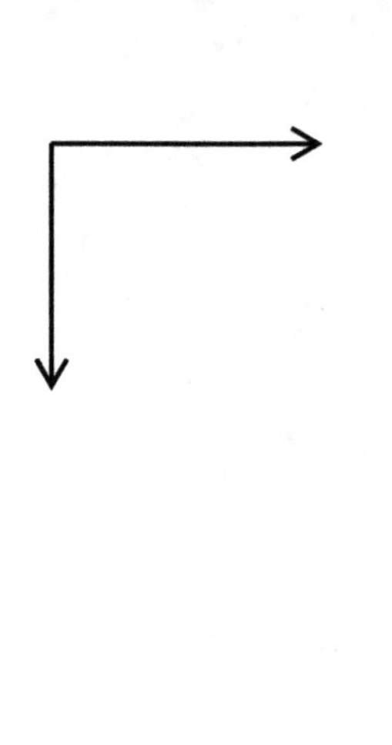

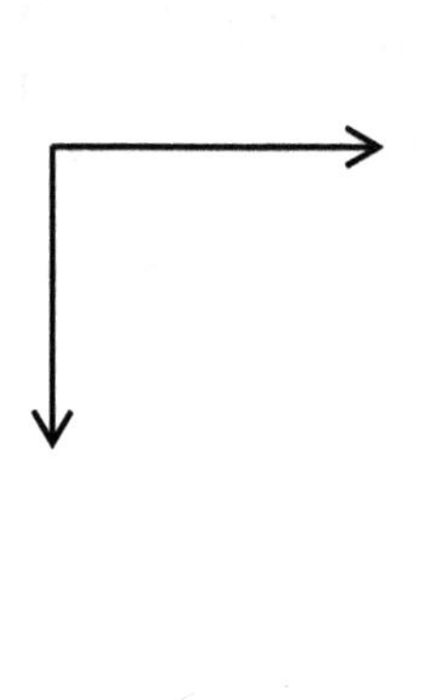

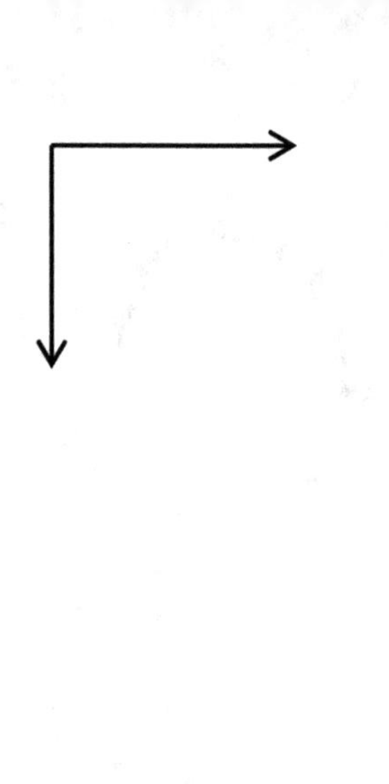

HAPPY COLORING

www.ingramcontent.com/pod-product-compliance
Lightning Source LLC
Chambersburg PA
CBHW081340160726
48000CB00010B/3179